Discerning Welcome

Discerning Welcome

A Reformed Faith Approach to Refugees

Ellen Clark Clémot

CASCADE *Books* • Eugene, Oregon

DISCERNING WELCOME
A Reformed Faith Approach to Refugees

Copyright © 2022 Ellen Clark Clemot. All rights reserved. Except for brief quotations in critical publications or reviews, no part of this book may be reproduced in any manner without prior written permission from the publisher. Write: Permissions, Wipf and Stock Publishers, 199 W. 8th Ave., Suite 3, Eugene, OR 97401.

Cascade Books
An Imprint of Wipf and Stock Publishers
199 W. 8th Ave., Suite 3
Eugene, OR 97401

www.wipfandstock.com

PAPERBACK ISBN: 978-1-6667-0892-9
HARDCOVER ISBN: 978-1-6667-0893-6
EBOOK ISBN: 978-1-6667-0894-3

Cataloguing-in-Publication data:

Names: Clemot, Ellen Clark, author.

Title: Discerning welcome : a Reformed faith approach to refugees / Ellen Clark Clemot.

Description: Eugene, OR: Cascade Books, 2022 | Includes bibliographical references and index.

Identifiers: ISBN 978-1-6667-0892-9 (paperback) | ISBN 978-1-6667-0893-6 (hardcover) | ISBN 978-1-6667-0894-3 (ebook)

Subjects: LCSH: Refugees—Religious aspects—Christianity. | Immigrants—Government policy—United States. | Emigration and Immigration—Religious aspects—Christianity.

Classification: BR517 C60 2022 (print) | BR517 (ebook)

03/15/22

Scripture quotations are from New Revised Standard Version Bible, copyright © 1989 National Council of Churches in the United States of America. Used by permission. All rights reserved worldwide.

To André-Louis, Annabelle, and Amélie

Contents

Acknowledgments | ix
Prologue | xi
Introduction | xiii

Part 1: Arriving as an Undocumented Refugee | 1

1 The Morality of Border Walls and the New Cosmopolitanism | 3

2 Bare Life and the Reformed Faith Perspective on Refugees | 27

Part 2: Residing as an Undocumented Refugee | 37

3 State Sovereignty and the Rights of the Resident Alien | 39

4 The Sovereignty of God and the Polity of the Common Good | 61

Part 3: Abiding with the Undocumented Refugee | 73

5 A Christian Ethic of Worship, Witness, and Welcome | 75

6 Sanctuary Church, Civil Disobedience, or Lawful Advocacy? | 87

Conclusion | 103
Epilogue | 107
Bibliography | 109

Acknowledgments

I AM DEEPLY GRATEFUL to the congregations of the Presbyterian Church of Chatham Township and of the Larchmont Avenue Church for their generosity in supporting my research and allowing me time to complete the writing of this book. I am especially grateful for the unwavering support of Larchmont elders Marjorie Lindblom and Kim Christiansen, and for trustee Barbara Flickinger who graciously agreed to read and comment on an early draft, and to Chatham's clerk of session Maury Gately and Chatham elders Martin Barbato and Carl Woodward, who read through the final one. I am honored that these two churches made refugee welcome a priority in their local community context as part of our ministry together.

I am also thankful for my many academic advisors along the way, including Duke Divinity School professors Luke Bretherton, Stanley Hauerwas, and Will Willimon. Their kindness and intellectual generosity helped me bring this book to light from what began as a transformational experience in my church ministry. I am also grateful for the thoughtfulness of Colin Yuckman, who helped me make connections among scholars in the Reformed tradition even as he establishes his place among them.

In researching this book, I was very fortunate to meet Rev. Dr. Donald K. McKim and am grateful for his ongoing interest and encouragement in my research and writing. He kindly introduced me to Professor Kenneth Woo, of Pittsburgh Theological

Acknowledgments

Seminary, who pointed me in the right direction for finding historical perspectives on the Reformed faith and the life of John Calvin as a religious refugee. It was a privilege to share in their scholarly fellowship and our mutual Reformed tradition.

Finally, I want to express my deepest gratitude to my family for their patient support of my newfound ministry and encouragement of my writing. With love, I dedicate this work to my husband, André, and our daughters, Annabelle and Amélie. For the precious treasure of each of them, I give thanks to God.

Ellen Clark Clemot
Princeton, August 2021

Prologue

On a gray, cold weekday morning in late January 2018, Roby, an Indonesian refugee residing in the US, and a quiet, friendly, and deeply faithful family man, was arrested by Immigration and Customs Enforcement (ICE) agents after dropping off his daughter at the local public high school in New Jersey. He was taken to central booking and detained on charges of residing in the US without an immigrant visa. ICE agents then transported him to a windowless detention center east of Newark, near the industrial waterfront where shipping containers sit in endless rows. If he could have looked outside, he would have seen the Statue of Liberty standing with her back to him.

Roby had resided illegally in the US for twenty years. He first arrived in America fleeing persecution as a Christian from his home in Indonesia, a predominantly Muslim nation with a track record of violent persecution of people of other faiths. When Roby arrived in the US, he had a nonimmigrant tourist visa. He did not know that he had one year to apply for asylum and seek resident alien status. When he finally tried to apply, it was already too late. He hired a lawyer to help remedy the situation, but his case was mishandled, and Roby's asylum claim foundered.

Roby found himself in an impossible situation. To renew his asylum case after the deadline had passed, he would have to leave the country for ten years and reapply from outside the US—but that would mean returning to Indonesia, the country where people

Prologue

had threatened his life, burned down his church, and murdered his pastor. It also meant leaving his Indonesian wife and US-born daughters behind—or taking them with him into danger. He chose what seemed to be the only realistic option: remain in the US illegally, and out of sight from ICE agent sweeps, while he continued with his job as a third-shift forklift operator at a local factory. He provided for his family, paid his US taxes, worshipped with an Indonesian community at a mainline Presbyterian church, and did the best he could to make a life for his family in America.

At the time of his arrest, I was serving as interim pastor at the church where Roby was a member—where he had served as a deacon and had his children baptized. I knew Roby only as a quiet man of deep faith. I had no idea that he was undocumented until I learned of his arrest. The entire congregation was shocked, along with me, to hear the news. We gathered for a prayer vigil at church. We rallied at town hall. The surrounding community rallied with us. The news media came. State legislators, US congressmen, the mayor—everyone assembled to express their outrage. The town erupted in indignation that one of their own, a good neighbor in town for over twenty years, devoted father, church member, friend, was behind bars because of his visa status. The neighborhood recognized that something was morally wrong. And yet, despite the prayers, and the rallies, and the politicians, and the news media, Roby remained in jail. For months and months.

I visited Roby in prison. I brought him church bulletins, newsletters, notes from his wife, and whatever nuggets of hope I could smuggle into jail through the bread of the Eucharist and the pages of his Indonesian Bible. In our conversations, he shared his dreams for the day he would be released. Every time he would enter the special consultation cell where we would meet near the prisoner dorms, he beamed with gratitude to have a visitor. His eyes always teared up. But he never lost hope.

Introduction

THE GOAL OF THIS book is to help congregants and churches to discern an ethical path to welcoming the stranger, specifically the long-term resident, undocumented refugee. Discerning welcome for the refugee involves an assessment of our political life together as a faith community, of the political and humanitarian needs of lives that are in danger, and a commitment to mercy as taught to us by Christ. And because every church community has its own context and its own community of refugees, it is for each church to discern the appropriate welcome to offer our neighbor refugees in ways that are both life-giving for the neighbor and promote peace for all.

In the pages that follow, I will address the ethical issues facing church leaders and congregants in welcoming undocumented refugees who seek to remain in residence in the US. And I will use the Presbyterian-Reformed faith tradition as our guide along the way. Our process of discernment follows a three-part path as we assess (i) the morality of border walls with regard to the human and political needs of the refugee, (ii) the legal rights, political life, and moral obligations of the nation-state and the church, and (iii) the ethical obligations of individual church members and churches towards refugees in our shared *polis*. In learning about the ethics of immigration and political theology, and by connecting with refugees through worship, witness, and welcome, congregants can begin to establish relationships with their refugee neighbors and offer ethical, legal, and redemptive ways of including them in our common life together.

But how do we assist undocumented resident refugees as we live out our Christian faith, when segments of our society call for their removal? How do we offer them neighbor love when US policy is set on sending undocumented residents back to their countries of origin? As a policy matter, if refugees somehow enter and reside in the US illegally, but peacefully, over time, should they be removed? Or does their long-term residence change things? These are the questions I seek to answer from a Christian ethics and Reformed faith perspective in this book. I do not recommend that congregants violate civil laws, but rather help refugees assess what actions are just and discern how to advocate for justice while following their Christian conscience in offering neighbor love to the refugee.

In applying an ethic of welcome to refugees, new questions arise. Can we, as Christians, prioritize our neighbor loves in a way that welcomes even the undocumented refugees living in our neighborhoods? Can we understand better why long-term undocumented resident refugees remain undocumented? How can we help them become full members of our society and feel fully human so they can flourish among us? To begin to find answers, it will help to understand how an undocumented refugee becomes a long-term resident of the US in the first place.

HOW LONG-TERM UNAUTHORIZED RESIDENCY OCCURS

Refugees who are long-term residents in the US, without authorized resident alien status, are typically people who have overstayed their nonimmigrant visas. These refugees want to apply for asylum. They want to become naturalized, legally documented residents as full members of society. But there is no legal mechanism to normalize their legal status. They often fly into the US from great distances and are initially given access to the country legally, and temporarily, as tourists. But many non-English-speaking refugees

Introduction

arriving in the US are not aware of the one-year window to apply for asylum—or fail to understand the procedures to follow when their tourist visas expire. If arriving refugees follow the procedure on how to be recognized as "legal" refugees upon arrival, or soon thereafter, they could be set on a pathway to US citizenship. But many refugees make tragic procedural missteps upon their arrival in the US, with irreversible consequences.

HOW UNDOCUMENTED IMMIGRANTS MOST RECENTLY BECAME TARGETS OF SUSPICION

Before the terrorist attacks on America that took place on September 11, 2001, undocumented immigrant refugees were tolerated and largely ignored by the US government. After 9/11, undocumented immigrants from predominantly Muslim countries were tracked down and rounded up by ICE, which was newly minted as a division of Homeland Security. As post-9/11 intolerance and wariness of immigrant Muslims grew, ICE asked for voluntary registration by all undocumented immigrants, especially from countries with predominantly Muslim populations.

The experience of the immigrant community where Roby lived in New Jersey was typical. The men of this large, mainly undocumented, Christian Indonesian refugee group, including Roby, decided to register with ICE. They thought that by registering they would earn amnesty and a better chance of remaining in the US—that it was a first step towards regularizing their non-visa status and making them "legal." But the reverse happened. The registration system that ICE offered turned out to be a tracking method and marked them as permanent outlaws.

From then on, the registrants were all identified as being present in the US without authorization and had to report to ICE every six months. They were initially allowed to remain as undocumented residents without any adjudication of their refugee or immigrant status. They were never granted visas, but they were silently permitted to work and were able to obtain driver's licenses. They continued to pay their taxes and make Social Security

Introduction

contributions. They continued to reside in the US under a voluntary surveillance system. The men's wives, who never registered in order to stay safely in the shadows to care for their children, were neither discovered nor pursued. But the men became easy targets for ICE arrests as immigration policies hardened over time.

Since 2008, under both Democrat and Republican administrations, the federal government has cracked down on undocumented immigrants and increased the number of their "removals" (the administrative policy term for deportations), especially of undocumented aliens with criminal records. But the easiest arrests to make were the undocumented refugees who had registered with ICE. They had volunteered their home address, work whereabouts, and phone numbers. They were the first to go. And yet they were also the most civilly responsible—the ones with jobs and savings, the ones with homes and families, the ones, like Roby, who worshipped God and raised their children in the community as Americans.

Negative messaging about undocumented refugees living within the US overlooks their civic and fiscal contributions to US society. Anti-immigrant politicians villainize the undocumented refugee for unsubstantiated wrongs, or contend that the isolated wrongdoing of one applies to all. Congregants who seek both an orderly, peaceful society and socially responsible immigrant neighbors have grown confused about immigration justice. They want to help people in need, but they don't want to welcome criminals. Yet being undocumented is not a crime; it is a civil wrong only. We have all seen hardworking, honest immigrants in our own neighborhoods. Many of us are immigrants ourselves. Yet when the US government targets undocumented aliens for arrest and removal, it tends to demonize the entire group, even those who have always been good neighbors, individuals contributing to the good of all.

There is confusion about where the truth lies, what the laws say, and what long-term undocumented refugees have been doing in the US all this time. Misunderstanding leads many congregants to wait out the conflict on the sidelines. Citizens and society members, who have the comfort of already belonging, have grown

Introduction

weary of the vociferous, televised ICE arrests of undocumented people, and the images of crowded detention centers housing unauthorized migrants along the southern border. The steady stream of asylum-seekers seems never ending.

The conflict over whether to welcome unauthorized refugees living in our communities or send them back to their country of origin can sound purely political, and in a certain sense it is. But for churches and their congregations, the resolution of the conflict depends on how they frame their theological reflections. A just Christian immigration ethic should provide a consistent civic and religious response to the undocumented refugee in need of neighbor love. In the pages that follow, I present a Reformed faith framework for ethical discernment that will help congregants and their churches find such an ethic to live by.

A NARROW FOCUS ON THE UNDOCUMENTED REFUGEE

To focus this inquiry, I examine only one isolated aspect of US immigration policy: the long-term resident, undocumented refugee seeking asylum in the US. I will not consider the situation of all immigrants to the US, but only those who are refugees seeking asylum. This focus provides the most compelling case for welcome and a starting place for further reflection on other immigration scenarios.

"Refugees" are people seeking a place of safety and refuge from their home countries where their lives are threatened by such dangers as violent gangs or civil unrest, religious persecution, or racial genocide. It seems natural and humane to assist people who fled other countries because their lives were in danger. Such a neighbor in need is a "refugee," as defined by the United Nations in its Convention on Refugees. In abbreviated form, the Convention states:

> [A refugee is] a person who is outside his country of nationality or habitual residence; has a well-founded fear of persecution because of his race, religion, nationality, membership in a particular social group, or political

Introduction

opinion; and is unable or unwilling to avail himself of the protection of that country, or return there, for fear of persecution.[1]

Refugees are a protected group given special consideration when seeking access to any UN signatory nation-state, such as the United States. US immigration laws and policies give such special consideration to the refugee so long as the refugee follows the appropriate asylum-seeker procedures. In this book, I use the word *refugee* to describe asylum-seekers. The resident aliens living in the US with "refugee status" have, by definition, authorization to reside in the US. They, too, need neighbor welcome in their community, and the ethical case for offering it is strongest as they have the legal right to remain but are often discriminated against for reasons of bias and fear. The legal category of refugee in the US applies to those people who applied to the State Department for refuge in the US from abroad. It is the undocumented asylum-seeker whose plight is covered here, people I describe as "undocumented refugees," people needing protection, and the most vulnerable to being expelled without authorization to reside in the US.

Because I am interested in assisting churches and congregants to choose to welcome the undocumented refugees already living in their communities, the method of entry into the US of these migrants is irrelevant to my analysis. Some undocumented refugees enter the US by an illegal border crossing. More typically, undocumented refugees who were once legally admitted to the US on nonimmigrant visas have become undocumented aliens by the passage of time. When they overstay the duration of a temporary visa permit, these aliens automatically become undocumented—out of compliance with US immigration laws—and then must live lives that are relatively invisible and without many of the social benefits or civil rights that citizenship would bring.

I focus on the unique aspects of the life of the refugee. I do not address the related cases of the economic immigrant or non-asylum-seeker, migrants fleeing the devastating effects of climate

---

1. UNHCR, "Convention on Refugees," Art. 1.

Introduction

change on their homes or their means of livelihood, or any visa applicants who are filtered out by US border controls. Instead, I attend to the longer-term resident, undocumented refugee (whether or not having officially applied for asylum in the US)—the person that congregants are most likely to meet in their day-to-day lives. This narrow focus can help congregants to make ethical decisions about neighbor interaction and welcome of refugees in their own communities today as a first step towards reflection on expressing neighbor love for a broader group in the future.

It can be difficult to distinguish the economically motivated flight of certain migrants to the US from refugees fleeing physical harm or persecution. But only those immigrants who have, or would self-describe as having, refugee status will be part of my analysis. An extension of this work could readily cover the claims of economically motivated migrants for entry, but their case does not avail itself to remedies provided to the refugee as currently set out in US immigration laws. Refugee "asylum status" is a legal category authorizing immediate entry for refugees and residence in the US if all conditions are met, including the condition that there is a threat to their lives if they were returned home.

Another issue that I will not address is the failure of the US immigration system to process asylum-seekers and other migrants arriving at the US borders in a prompt and humane way. Many asylum-seekers are held in detention centers, separated from their minor children, or are children themselves, and are ill-treated by a system that has not kept up with the numbers of applicants seeking a home in America. These are important issues for future study, but the focus of my inquiry is limited to how faithful Christians should act towards the undocumented refugee already residing in their communities—people who have already been neighbors for a long time.

Introduction

EQUIPPING CONGREGATIONS FOR NEIGHBORLINESS TO REFUGEES

The goal of this book is to equip congregants and churches to resolve questions, especially from a Reformed faith perspective, of how and whether to welcome long-term resident, undocumented refugees in their communities. Is it ethical for churches and congregations to welcome undocumented refugees in a nation-state when there are laws discouraging it? I offer help with the moral decision-making process from learnings in political theology and Christian ethics so that congregants can take faithful action towards refugees in response. My central claim is that, despite the existence of border walls, or because of them, churches and congregants can construct a peaceful political community with the undocumented resident refugee in the US by implementing a Christian ethic of hospitality, one that is grounded in mercy, and offers a welcoming connection to the broader society, through implementing God's call to loving our neighbor refugees.

Through the application of a just Christian immigration ethic, described as a "new cosmopolitanism," and rescuing the resident, undocumented refugee from a meager existence as "bare life" through acceptance into society, and through offering welcoming interactions as neighbors, congregants can connect with resident refugees in their own cities and towns and build a flourishing community together. Congregants pursuing a Christian ethic of immigration, one that they have discerned in response to the call of Christ on their own lives, while recognizing the needs of the refugee in their own communities, can make a positive difference in the lives of everyone, undocumented refugee and citizen alike. The undocumented refugee can provide an equally positive influence on the life of the congregation as well.

Through acts of worship, witness, and welcome, congregants can grow in their discipleship by becoming neighbors, coming face-to-face with the undocumented refugee who resides among them, and offering hospitality through neighborliness. Pursuing this just Christian ethic of immigration to its legitimate end means

Introduction

making changes in law and policy so that the resident refugee can one day become a US citizen in our *polis*, no longer the other, but at long last, one of us.

THE BIBLICAL, ETHICAL, AND POLITICAL BASIS FOR DISCERNMENT

Christ's mission for Christ followers to love God and love neighbor is deeply political. When the neighbor we discover among us is a refugee, lacking legal status but seeking safety and security in our *polis*, the Christian has a *political* decision to make: whether or not to follow Christ by welcoming the refugee into the community as God's own creation and a neighbor in need. The pages that follow will provide a framework for such political decision-making and practical methods for churchgoers to embrace immigration politics as Christian ethicists.

Scripture teaches us to love our neighbor, especially the resident alien among us. Yet, increasingly xenophobic rhetoric in the US against undocumented resident alien refugees requires an act of courage for Christians to stand up for the refugee. How we live as Christians in the *polis*, as a people who practice mercy, compassion, and forgiveness, requires our courage for a reason. As Stanley Hauerwas and Will Willimon first pointed out in their landmark book *Resident Aliens,* some thirty years ago, Christians are themselves, metaphorically speaking, "resident aliens" living in a strange, secular land. We find the world opposed to what God is leading us to do—living a life centered around Jesus as Christ, sharing together as a community. The church community is more like a faith colony, they argue, than a mere congregation—it inhabits a secular world like a "stranger living in a strange place."[2]

The larger responsibility of Christians, to their faith and to their non-Christian neighbors, points to the *telos*, or end, of Christian life in community: to witness to the world that God is busy redeeming, bringing all humanity back into relationship with God

2. Hauerwas and Willimon, *Resident Aliens*, 78.

Introduction

through Jesus Christ. Living out our faith means keeping constant attention to God's reconciling work around us, and playing a part in that reconciliation where we can. For some, living a Christian life can set us at odds with secular society. But ideally, living out our faith leads us to reconcile our ethical beliefs with our societal conduct, lifting up social interactions with the stranger where a rudderless world weighs them down.

Teaching ways to live out a Christ-centered life, Hauerwas and Willimon maintain that "the way for the world to know that it is broken and fallen, is for the church to enable the world to strike hard against something that is alternative to what the world offers."[3] Christian ethics offers this alternative—a Christ-centered approach of how to act and what to do in face of a fallen world. Embracing the refugee as a welcome member of society is Christian witness to Christ's teaching, and a political choice in the sense of living a public life that dares to see the stranger as a neighbor, and the Good Samaritan as a role model.

In pursuing the common good in public life, as followers of Christ, be it in safety and security, health and welfare, or immigration policies, we are engaging in both a religious and political act. Stanley Hauerwas calls this missional work the very politics of salvation, with its *telos* as Christ.[4] Applying Christian ethics to immigration issues, congregants can choose to practice a theology of hospitality: welcoming our nearby neighbor refugees as friends in the common pursuit of community flourishing. Our theological goal, to welcome the stranger in the name of Christ, becomes our *political* goal. When our politics become aligned with following Christ, the practices of our daily lives and the focus of our churches' missional commitments become more clearly expressions of our Christian faith.

Christian ethicist Luke Bretherton describes the politics of welcome in this way: "Christian hospitality . . . pertains to politics because it is a way of conceptualizing how to forge a common life—that is, a public life—with others with whom we disagree or

3. Hauerwas and Willimon, *Resident Aliens*, 94.
4. Hauerwas, *After Christendom*, 27.

Introduction

who are, at some level, strangers to us."[5] As we forge this common life together, Christian ethics, hospitality, and political theology can help provide a framework to manage the tension between living our faith and sharing a public life with others. This approach to life together in community also provides a guide to churches on how to welcome the undocumented neighbor who is a long-term resident refugee.

A METHODOLOGY OF REFORMED FAITH AND CHRISTIAN ETHICS

The method I propose for discerning an ethical framework for Christian decision-making relies on the Reformed faith tradition's touchstones of scriptural authority, creedal confessions, and our response to God's ongoing work of creation in our social-historical context—the context of our everyday lives as it relates to the refugee. I focus on two influential themes in Reformed theology in particular: (i) the Doctrine of the Covenant, with its corresponding declaration of the freedoms of humanity before God to love our neighbors far and near, and (ii) the creedal Confessions of the Reformed churches, with primary attention to the Declaration of Barman, with related theological writings of Karl Barth. As a Reformed theologian, Barth developed the idea that the role of a Christian community is to advise the nation-state of its true purposes to defend human freedom, hope, and justice, while the Christian community must also defend the dignity and rights of humanity and serve both as guardian and witness to the kingdom of God.[6] These themes will guide our process of discernment ahead.

In choosing to apply the Reformed faith tradition and its scriptural, confessional, and social contexts as the method for this study, I attempt to reclaim the relevancy of the church, particularly churches in the Presbyterian-Reformed tradition, in addressing urgent social justice matters facing our individual lives

---

5. Bretherton, *Christianity and Contemporary Politics*, 19.
6. Barth, *Community*, 38, 41–42.

Introduction

in community. As Reformed theologian Shirley Guthrie argued in response to the tension he described as a "crisis" for churches trying to remain relevant to modern society while retaining their identity as Christian, we already have the tools at hand necessary to bring a faithful, ethical response to the problems of our day. Guthrie wrote:

> I believe that Christians in the Presbyterian-Reformed tradition do not have to look around for a new theological base to deal with the crisis. They have only to take their own confessional heritage seriously, for in it respect for the authority of scripture, respect for Christian tradition, and faithful response to historical-cultural context are inextricably related in a way that both requires and enables an understanding of Christian faith and life that is at once authentically Christian and at the same time open to dialogue and fellowship with fellow Christians and others who are different from us in a pluralistic church and world.[7]

Thus, in aligning with Guthrie, I look to Scripture as authoritative, to creedal statements as relevant guidance, and to our current context of concerns for the refugee as impetus enough to move us forward with an ethical plan of action for churches and congregations. The Reformed tradition embraces a Christian theology that is "reformed and always being reformed—in the light of God's Word,"[8] such that it welcomes new ideas and practices that share in Christ's free gift of grace and teaching of merciful neighborliness.

Reformed theology is particularly useful in grappling with current issues of social justice. It is open to changes in practice while being true to the underlying theological theme of God's prior initiative and our gracious response. The Presbyterian-Reformed faith tradition understands God as a benevolent God who created us and all the world, and first gave us love and the gift of grace through Jesus Christ.[9] The Reformed tradition encourages Chris-

---

7. Guthrie Jr., *Always Being Reformed*, 12.
8. McKim, *Presbyterian Faith*, 90.
9. McKim, *Introducing the Reformed Faith*, 179.

Introduction

tians to see themselves as grateful recipients moved to respond to God and others with acts of kindness, love, and mercy. Together, God's initiative and our response to God provides a basis for our own behavior of benevolence towards our neighbor refugee. Applying these distinctive elements of Reformed theology to our Christian life practices will be part of my methodology in addressing the challenge of refugee welcome for churches in the US today.

I also provide a comparative look at other theological and philosophical perspectives that contribute to a just Christian immigration ethic. I present the viewpoints of Catholic Social Teaching and of political philosophers who offer compelling insights and strategies on refugee welcome and restraint. In surveying these viewpoints, I distinguish how the Reformed tradition sometimes differs from, or merges with these approaches, so as to provide a road map of ethical thinking for congregants and churches in the Reformed tradition to follow, and for other Christians to consider, as they discern their own ethical approach to immigration justice and refugee welcome in the United States.

Writing as a pastor, Christian ethicist, practical theologian, and lawyer, I hope to provide churchgoers with touch-points to help understand the needs of the refugee, the legitimate rights and responsibilities of the nation-state, the sovereignty of God, and the responsibilities of Christians to both *polis* and person. In writing this book, I offer answers to the question that many faithful congregants ask: "What should be my Christian response to the presence of undocumented refugees in my neighborhood?" With a just Christian immigration ethic in place, congregants can better decide for themselves how to act as Christians in the voting booth, in the public square, and in their life's work as Christian disciples in the communities in which they live.

HELPFUL DEFINITIONS FOR TERMS USED IN THIS BOOK

Christian immigration ethics helps us discern how to respect the rights and obligations both of the nation-state in which we reside

Introduction

as citizens and of the neighbor undocumented refugees whom the church calls us to love. "Ethics" are ways of doing and acting—how we respond to the decisions we face every day. "Christian ethics" are the ways we respond and act in light of the Christian story—with a particular set of virtues and an ultimate end goal of reconciling with God through Christ. "Immigration ethics" are the ways we determine our action plan regarding people who enter our country by crossing our borders.

"Political theology" provides a way of thinking about "politics" that is not steeped in a partisan shouting match, but rather offers an understanding of the rights and obligations of the nation-state and the inhabitants of it. "Politics" is the life of the community living together in the *polis*—a sovereign entity that provides safety and security to its members, and has the power, and the right, to exclude others from entering. The Reformed tradition's attitude towards the communal *polis* is one of shared harmony, an acknowledgment that to live together we need earthly rules and magistrates and enforcement powers for the preservation of peace, and for participation in God's promised future.

The "political" for purposes of this book is, thus, that which relates to the *polis* and the lives of everyone living in that community or trying to access it. *Polis* is sometimes used here as interchangeable with the word "nation-state" meaning a sovereign, self-governed secular entity with rights over its own territory and the ingress and egress of people through it. The *polis* can be a country, a city, or the town in which we live.

I use the term "resident undocumented refugees" rather than "illegal resident aliens" because not all resident aliens are refugees, or in the US illegally. Moreover, I avoid the term "illegal alien" as it has the misleading connotation that the alien is somehow criminal *per se*. As will be developed in part 2, the "undocumented" resident is not an "illegal" person, but rather one who resides in the US without authorization. Being undocumented is an illegal, prohibited status, but it does not define a person's moral character or impinge on one's standing as a beloved creature in the eyes of God.

Introduction

A "resident alien" is the noncitizen living in a host country—much like the biblical stranger in a strange land. Resident aliens are subject to and beneficiaries of alienage laws that apply to resident noncitizens. US alienage laws are often in tension with immigration laws—sometimes the two conflict. After years, even decades, of living in the US, undocumented resident alien refugees have usually become embedded in the social fabric of their communities. They benefit from alienage laws, but, as undocumented refugees, they have no means of becoming citizens of the United States or full beneficiaries of the laws and freedoms that US citizens enjoy.

OVERVIEW OF THE CHAPTERS IN THIS BOOK

The book is divided into three parts, each with two chapters, to take the reader from conceptual ethics about border walls to practical solutions for interacting with undocumented refugee neighbors. Each part is a step along the journey to inclusion, from border wall to church sanctuary.

Part 1 presents the challenges of arriving at the edge of asylum as a refugee. Chapter 1 sets out the ethical debate about border walls. Conceptually it addresses inclusion in, and exclusion from, a bordered territory and participation in a local *polis* based on theological beliefs and political behaviors. The chapter concludes that the refugee is owed a special duty of care that demands welcome, a political solution that can be expressed in a "new cosmopolitanism," recognizing borders as a place of interface with the stranger in communion with God. Chapter 2 explores the lived reality of the refugee stripped of political rights and the problematic impact on the refugee when humanitarian aid is disconnected from the political life of the nation-state. Applying the experience of John Calvin as an example, I close the chapter with a look at refugee welcome in Calvin's Geneva, and refugee welcome as an expression of neighborliness today.

Part 2 turns to an exploration of the laws of the nation-state and the laws of God as applied to the undocumented refugee. As

Introduction

a starting place, chapter 3 presents the conflicts and ambiguities inherent in US immigration and alienage laws that impact the lives of long-term resident, undocumented refugees. The chapter also looks at the legal and political problems that arise for the refugee who has been deemed "stateless." Chapter 4 considers the situation of the refugee under the sovereignty of God. I introduce Augustinian concepts of the earthly city within the kingdom of God and the shared goal of citizen and refugee for a peaceful community in which to live and flourish. The chapter concludes with Augustine's "ordered loves" that encourage care of those neighbors in need, especially those living nearby, such as the neighbor refugee.

Part 3 offers a practical theology of welcome. It begins at chapter 5 with practical guidance on neighbor welcome for churches and congregants. It explores worship as a method of church welcome through liturgy, sermon, and sacrament, and then moves to public witness through advocacy, outreach, and community fellowship. Chapter 6 considers sanctuary church and civil disobedience as an ethical option for certain congregations, and other forms of advocacy in compliance with the law as an ethical option for others. I conclude the chapter with a call to action for congregants and churches to discern their path forward and make strides in welcoming the resident undocumented refugee living in their own neighborhoods.

My hope is that this book will equip readers with new ways to think ethically about the political issue of refugee welcome and to choose mercy as a way of life.

Part 1
Arriving as an Undocumented Refugee

Chapter 1

The Morality of Border Walls and the New Cosmopolitanism

> "For [Christ Jesus] is our peace; . . . [he] has broken down the dividing wall, that is, the hostility between us."
>
> —Eph 2:14 (NRSV)

INTRODUCTION

ARE BORDER WALLS IMMORAL?—OR needful? How do we decide? This chapter embarks on a conversation with Christian ethicists about the morality of border walls that hinder the refugee's access to asylum in a peaceful nation-state. Many of the ethicists studied here follow the Reformed tradition in their reasoning. Others privilege the response of Catholic Social Teaching, while we will also hear from others who are political philosophers. I will point out the differences and why they matter to congregations and churches, especially for those in the Reformed tradition,

Part 1: Arriving as an Undocumented Refugee

discerning how best to welcome the long-term resident undocumented refugee already living in their communities.

The debate on borders will help us understand ways to think ethically about community membership behind those walls, and access to membership by refugees as an exceptionally vulnerable group. Even as we examine the plight of the refugee outside the walls looking in, we will also consider the rights and privileges of those on the inside looking out. Basing our priorities on an understanding of God's desire for human flourishing in communion with God and one another, we will develop a Reformed Christian immigration ethic that respects the common cause of refugee and nation-state to promote an earthly peace.

In discussing the morality of border walls, I first define the spectrum of ethical responses to refugee claims for asylum, and the corresponding duty of care that arises for a nation-state regarding people seeking asylum. I then explore the concept and consequences of national border walls as a defining reality for both the nation-state, in securing its territory and creating an orderly *polis*, and the refugee, who seeks protection and belonging within those same walls. I conclude this chapter by recommending a middle way, consonant with Reformed theology and its expression of covenant theology and mercy for the neighbor in need, to maintain border walls, not as either open or closed, but rather as the nation-state's interface with God's creation.

Putting Border Walls in Perspective—the *Telos* of Christ

For Christian ethicists, the debate around borders, refugees, asylum-seekers, and the sovereign rights of nation-states ultimately ties into our overall relationship with God. According to Christian ethicist Luke Bretherton, politics is central to the moral discussion around living a good and flourishing life—not only our own, but also how our lives intersect with others. He writes:

> Politics determines whether this common life is just or unjust, generous or heartless, peaceable or violent . . . Unsurprisingly then, from the Bible onward, political life

The Morality of Border Walls and the New Cosmopolitanism

has figured largely in theological reflection on the meaning, purpose, and ordering of human life in response to the revelation of God given in Jesus Christ.[1]

As we navigate the realities of our common life together, in the context in which we find ourselves, both theology and politics will inform the moral decisions we make and the ethical actions we take as followers of Christ. All aspects of our efforts to ensure a place of asylum for the refugee, while maintaining the sovereignty and stability of the nation-state, require our constant attention to following our *telos*, our ultimate goal, of reconciliation with God through promoting an earthly peace.

UNDERSTANDING BORDERED TERRITORIES AND THE PLIGHT OF THE REFUGEE

Although the long-term undocumented resident refugee is not a new arrival, the border wall, when confronted by the refugee, whether physically at the edges of the nation-state, or symbolically at passport control in an airport, is a helpful starting place for the ethical inquiry around the question of "who's in and who's out?" It has undeniable echoes of Christ's judgment of humanity at the end of times, and for some refugees, gaining access to refuge can feel just as salvific.

International law norms provide that people have the right to emigrate from their home country, but there is no accompanying right to enter someone else's country. Only the receiving nation-state can grant this privilege. There is no single answer to how refugee requests for entry should be treated. Policymakers need to consider and prioritize which outcomes are the most humane to the refugee, fair to citizens of the receiving nation, and mutually satisfactory to all parties. As the purpose of this chapter is to help congregants be able to think about borders ethically, we will start by recognizing, and navigating around, differing but ethically defensible points of view.

---

1. Bretherton, *Christ and the Common Life*, 18.

Part 1: Arriving as an Undocumented Refugee

Two Competing Ethical Viewpoints on International Migration

Immigration policy addresses the movement of people across the territorial boundaries of nation-states. Scholars have developed paradigms to describe ways of thinking about the international migration of people across these borders. The two most influential theories of international migration, that have a moral element to them, are referred to by ethicists as "communitarianism"—which understands the world as a community of states that are structured by power, morality, and law; and "cosmopolitanism"—which conceptualizes a single, equitable world community and gives political preference to the rights of the individual within it. Although both views attempt to promote human dignity of the migrant, and recognize a duty of care to the refugee, the level of deference to the authority of the nation-state differs between them.

The two viewpoints result in very different approaches to immigration policy. Considering the two models in more reductionist terms, one could say that the cosmopolitan view favors more open borders and eschews the exclusionary tendency of nation-states as an impediment to social justice and the fair treatment of immigrants. It emphasizes the moral primacy of the global welfare of all people and views the sovereignty of nation-states as relatively unimportant.

By contrast, communitarianism views the existing community of states as normative, and, as Christian ethicist Mark Amstutz describes it, relies on political societies to secure human dignity and preserve human freedoms within the realm of, and subject to, the sovereignty of the nation-states.[2] From a communitarian perspective, in order to preserve sovereign authority and maintain social solidarity, the nation-state must necessarily regulate its borders. Yet border regulation need not be abandoned altogether in order to show mercy to one fleeing from harm. The special case of the refugee makes for exceptions to closed border policies because of the value of human life and the risk of death that haunts the refugee. Not surprisingly, what defines a person as a "refugee,"

2. Amstutz, *Just Immigration*, 82.

carrying a special privilege to entry into a bordered nation-state, is significant to the ethical determination of whether to allow entry to that stranger or to bar the door.

Understanding Refugees

Differentiating the "refugee" from other entrance-seekers is a significant moral step. Refugees are, by definition, in imminent danger of losing their lives if they remain in their home country. They need to find a place of safety and protection from the nation-state from which they flee. They also seek to join a stable, peaceful society governed by the rule of law, the thing they lacked at home. The refuge-seeker has already abandoned home because it is no longer a safe place in which to live. Refugees find themselves "betwixt and between," placeless, and homeless, constantly on the move.

The refugee's "placelessness" is another aspect of the refugee's difficult existence. People no longer able to stay safely in their home country, and seeking uncertain permission to enter other nation-states, are emotionally exhausted. Being constantly on the move, and on the lookout, complicates the life experience of refugees. Refugees are different from economic immigrants who seek a more prosperous way of life, or expatriates who are pursuing an employment opportunity that may be equally available in their home country. The refugee cannot stay home and survive, but rather must find a new sovereign polity and protector to call home. Refugees are uniquely those people fleeing persecution in their home country. They seek a new home in a peaceful, orderly, and secure host country.

According to Catholic Relief Services, over 244 million people reside in countries where they were not born. Another 65 million people have been forcibly displaced from their country of origin due to war, political repression, or religious persecution.[3] These

---

3. Collier et al., *Global Migration*, 8–9. The authors also note that these figures do not include the 22.5 million people displaced by the effects of natural disasters and climate change making it impossible for them to grow their crops and survive.

Part 1: Arriving as an Undocumented Refugee

displaced people are "refugees" as defined by the UN Convention on Refugees and are looking for a new place to live. US law distinguishes "asylum-seekers" as a related group seeking refuge. The asylum-seekers are individuals who arrive at the US border, or in a US airport, seeking asylum from the dangers of their homeland. But they must prove to US immigration authorities at their port of entry that they fear for their personal safety if they were to remain in their home countries. They can do this through a "credible fear" interview once inside the US. The individual then must apply for the status of an "asylum-seeker" and appear before an immigration law judge. Only if the judge's ruling is favorable may that person receive authorization to reside in the United States.

Other "asylum-seekers" who seek refuge in the US may have entered legally at first with a tourist visa, but then apply for asylum once inside the US and while in possession of that temporary visa permitting them to stay. According to immigration expert Roger Daniels, the refugee applies to gain access to the US for refuge from outside its borders, while still residing in a dangerous homeland. The asylum-seeker, on the other hand, also faces life-threatening danger back home, but is already on US soil when applying for refuge in the US.[4]

US-authorized "refugee" and "asylum status" both grant special rights to the person seeking refuge based on the nation-state's acknowledgement of the duty of care owed to the vulnerable victim of persecution. US immigration law also grants a path to citizenship for both refugees and asylees if they apply for "resident alien" status once admitted to the US. But the procedural steps can be difficult for applicants seeking asylum to understand and follow. As a result, many individuals seeking asylum in the US, who make it safely inside US territory, end up in the category of undocumented alien once they have resided in the US for one year and failed to apply for asylum or otherwise regularize their visa status.

For purposes of the discussions in this book, I use the term *refugee* to describe any individual fleeing his or her homeland due to life-threatening danger or persecution and who seeks refuge in

---

4. Daniels, *Guarding the Golden Door*, 204.

a different nation-state. This is far broader than US immigration law's definition of a "refugee" as someone who has been given permission to reside in the US after having applied for refugee status from abroad through the State Department. I use the term *undocumented refugee* to describe both (i) asylum-seekers in the US who have entered the US with non-refugee, temporary authorization, but have failed to comply with US immigration laws for permission to remain in residence in the US, and (ii) those asylum-seekers who have gained access to the US without entry authorization and continue to reside in the US without authorization to remain.

While US immigration law and policy requires undocumented immigrants who reside in the US to return to their native countries, as a general rule, international protocol restricts the ability of the US to do so in the case of undocumented refugees. The United Nation's Convention on the Status of Refugees of 1951 assured refugees receiving asylum a key protection: the right of *non-refoulement*. This means that a refugee, once inside the host country (UN member) territory, will *not* be returned to the country from which he or she fled.[5] The Convention acknowledges that each person who comes to the border seeking safety is one whose life is in danger. Yet, under US immigration law and policy, an unauthorized resident alien seeking asylum is not considered a "refugee" for purposes of applying the Convention. The ethical question surrounding refugee welcome then becomes not merely whether to allow the persecuted migrant in, but also, whether unauthorized refugees who penetrate the borders to reach asylum should be allowed to stay.

THE ETHICAL DEBATE BETWEEN COSMOPOLITANISM AND COMMUNITARIANISM

Border walls not only create ethical questions for citizens, they also create a paradox for the refugee. Walls are both sword and shield.

5. UNHCR, "Convention on Refugees," Art. 33.

Part 1: Arriving as an Undocumented Refugee

They both attract and repel, promise peace and protection, yet prevent entry to those in need of care. The refugee needs both an escape from harm at home and an entry into a different *polis* that offers a peaceful and orderly society governed by the rule of law. A strong nation-state beckons the refugee for its very promise of a peaceful community. Yet it maintains peace by enforcing civil laws which limit entry. And it requires a certain level of acquiescence by residents to the authority of the nation-state over its citizenry.

How we view border walls, then, as Christians wanting to provide hospitality, safety, and welcome to refugees, becomes a question of balancing access to outsiders while preserving stability within. Finding the right mix in this balance of human rights and sovereign rights is more art than science. In the US, immigration policies prioritizing one over the other have varied over time depending on the attitudes of Americans to immigration policy and to immigrants. Couching the debate as a theological one, Christian ethicists have staked out claims all along the spectrum of possibilities striving to expand God's peace in the ways we relate to one another, here and now.

The Case for No Borders—Cosmopolitanism

Some Christian ethicists support the elimination of borders altogether. Their arguments are primarily theological but also philosophical, despite the practical reality that our geopolitical world is divided up into bordered territories of nation-states. A leading light in this debate is Christian ethicist Joseph Carens, who was an early advocate for the cosmopolitan view of a world without borders and continues to be its most influential voice. Carens is a proponent of freedom of movement across borders, especially for the refugee. In his influential book *The Ethics of Immigration*, and in articles like "Aliens and Citizens," Carens makes his case. He argues that although refugees have "no claim to a political community," they may "nevertheless have a moral right to entry"—and,

The Morality of Border Walls and the New Cosmopolitanism

in his view, democratic states have an equally moral obligation to receive them.[6]

Carens emphasizes that the freedom to enter a host country and remain indefinitely is, or should be, a basic human right. In "Aliens and Citizens," Carens claims that borders should be as freely navigable for refugees as the freedom of movement for all people between cities and states is within the United States.[7] Although one could argue there is a moral distinctiveness and purpose for federal borders that differ from state borders as to movement of people, Carens's open borders view towards refugees remains influential to proponents of the cosmopolitan point of view.

Coming to a similar conclusion, but with a focus on the church universal as providing a borderless model of being, Christian ethicist Justin Ashworth asserts that Christians must actively witness against borders, as "God's people," summoned by Christ into solidarity with the most vulnerable.[8] He argues that Christians must build solidarity with vulnerable others, including non-Christians and the poor, across borders and in community. God blesses all people, Ashworth rightly claims, and Christ became a vulnerable person for us to join all things together through him—including refugees.

Ashworth recognizes that his rejection of nation-state borders can be seen as idealistic and naïve,[9] but he is emphatic in promoting an open welcome as a Christian response to the increasing numbers of refugees who have been refused entry to our borders. As a point of comparison, the Roman Catholic Church also takes a cosmopolitan approach to nation-states that encourages open borders for refugees, but not based on a universal "people of God" idea so much as recognition of Christ's mercy for the most destitute. Where Ashworth describes a preferential option for God's people, the Catholic church proclaims a preferential option for the poor.

---

6. Carens, *Ethics of Immigration*, 15.
7. Carens, "Aliens and Citizens," 266–67.
8. Ashworth, "Who Are Our People?," 506.
9. Ashworth, "Who Are Our People?," 498.

Part 1: Arriving as an Undocumented Refugee

Comparing Catholic Social Teaching: Preference for the Poor

The Roman Catholic Church encourages an open-border response to welcoming refugees as an expression of its Catholic Social Teaching. This open borders approach may be more practical than a no-borders position. Roman Catholic theologian William R. O'Neill, SJ, insists that this proposed view supports "porous borders" rather than none at all.[10] The concepts underlying Catholic Social Teaching as applied to immigration concerns include: human dignity, promotion of the common good, sharing of resources, and the preferential option for the poor.[11] It is the preferential option for the poor that makes Catholic Social Teaching distinctive, as well as providing a starting place for liberation theologians in focusing on society's most economically disadvantaged. Although I do not pursue liberation theology in this work, it is a direction to follow for other studies, especially regarding economically motivated immigration.

The *magna carta* on migrant welcome under Catholic Social Teaching came in the aftermath of World War II with the release of Pope Pius XII's constitutional document *Exsul familia*, promulgated in 1952.[12] *Exsul familia* (Exiled Family) gives instructions for the pastoral care of migrants. Its title refers to the Holy Family fleeing from Herod's rule to find safety in Egypt after the Christ child's birth. For the Catholic Church, the plight of the Holy Family became the archetype of every refugee family.

"A Pastoral Letter from the Catholic Bishops of Mexico and the United States" in 2003 applied Catholic Social Teaching to the migrants at our shared border and gave compassionate, though one-sided, faith-based guidance for immigration reform. The letter proposed five basic rights for refugees, including the right of refugees to find economic opportunities in their homeland or to migrate to another; the right to protection despite the sovereign's

---

10. O'Neill, "The Place of Displacement," 73.
11. Collier et al., *Global Migration*, 68.
12. Pope Pius XII, "Exsul Familia Nazarethana," 639–704.

right to control its borders; and the human right of dignity.[13] But this proposal has its flaws, especially for failing to recognize the rights of the receiving nation-states, and their obligations to their own citizenry.

One of the decisions churches and congregants must make is how to frame their approach to immigration decisions as a matter of Christian ethics. In thinking about helping their neighbors, congregants can be asking, as a matter of ethics: "Do refugees merit priority attention and automatic ingress at our borders?" and "Are there some neighbors who merit our attention more than others?" And regardless of theological stance, all Christians must ask the question raised in the parable of the Good Samaritan,[14] "Who is my neighbor?" when it comes time to show mercy towards the stranger in need.

Following a Reformed faith/Barthian approach, Christian ethicist Peter Meilaender introduces the idea of privileging special relationships in deciding whom we should help in the world of so many needy people. Meilaender might respond to the "Who is my neighbor?" question by answering: "It depends." He argues that the neighbor we are commanded to love is the one close by or present in our midst: the aging parent, the grieving widow, the fellow congregant who has lost his job. When we emphasize preferential treatment for the near at hand, we are making ethical decisions of a practical and rational sort—we have chosen to prioritize proximity of the needy, rather than attempt to assuage all the needy of the world, or only the poorest among them.[15]

The traditional cosmopolitan view of international relations rejects this idea of ordering or prioritizing people based on proximate relationships, but instead focuses on helping those most in need of help—wherever they may be. And as Carens points out, open-border theorists all view individuals as having equal moral worth—whether refugee or citizen. The thread that ties all these

---

13. Catholic Church and Conferencia del Episcopado Mexicano, eds., *Strangers No Longer*, 13–16.

14. Luke 10:25–37.

15. Meilaender, *Theory of Immigration*, 11.

Part 1: Arriving as an Undocumented Refugee

more liberal cosmopolitans together is the priority they give to individuals ahead of the community itself.

Similarly, philosopher Peter Singer,[16] an open-borders proponent, argues that the needs of a refugee, whose life is in danger, should take priority over the local citizen. And, as a result, border obstacles should fall away in order to provide the help needed, wherever it might be required. Singer values all lives equally but gives priority to the one bearing the greatest need, regardless of where that one in need resides.

Singer would agree with Carens's cosmopolitism and the Roman Catholic preference for the poor overall, but reemphasize the importance of assisting the global poor, people unable to reach our borders in the first place. In either case, both Carens and Singer, like Ashworth and the Catholic Bishops, are in the cosmopolitan camp—prioritizing the need to help one's neighbor—near or far, over the need to respect the sovereignty of one's homeland and its ability to exclude people at its borders. These cosmopolitan arguments should be part of the discernment process of our local churches and congregants who may never have considered border walls in quite these ways before.

Putting an emphasis on human rights and equality over sovereign interests are hallmarks of moral cosmopolitanism. For Christians, this view means that our commitment to our nation cannot outweigh our commitment to the human dignity of the worldwide community. Or, as another open-borders Christian ethicist, Tisha Rajendra, describes it, "the good of the nation-state cannot be secured at the expense of the human rights of immigrants."[17] She argues that Christian ethics insists on the "radical principle" that migrants are people—and have rights by their very humanity.

Like Meilaender, however, Rajendra notes that having rights does not necessarily mean that they create an equal and opposite responsibility for others. This was the flaw for the humanitarian-based arguments of the Catholic Bishops. They pursue the goal of human dignity without making a case for human justice. The

---

16. Singer, *One World*, 19.
17. Rajendra, *Migrants and Citizens*, 15.

"preferential option for the poor," although highly moral, is inadequate to counter questions of how to protect the rights of refugees while ensuring the preservation of the rights of citizens and the responsibilities of the nation-state.

In situations of such irresolvable conflict, sometimes grace is the answer. Joseph Carens suggests allowing the undocumented, long-term resident refugee to become a legal resident, or even a citizen, in the host country of asylum. One of his recommendations is to establish a time period after which such undocumented aliens could apply for legal residency. He proposes that after five years of living in the US, an undocumented refugee could apply for US citizenship. His policy approach is to provide an amnesty for undocumented aliens so that they can regularize their status after showing themselves to be contributing members of society with a desire to remain in the US. "It would be wrong to deport them once they have become members," Carens writes. "Over time, the circumstances of their entry become less important."[18] It is interesting to note that in this case Carens offers a preference for normalization to our nearest neighbor, the undocumented asylum-seeker already living in our midst. And yet, at the same time, he shares an egalitarian outlook with Singer, the philosopher who rejects near-neighbor privilege, but values everyone equally, near and far.

Congregants will need to assess their own context to discern whether to privilege care for near neighbors or those far away. The moral decisions we make can only ever be our best assessments of the information we have at hand in the varied situations where we find ourselves. Churches and congregants can give themselves an ounce of grace in acknowledging that the context in which they live will necessarily differ from other churches in other communities. Finding a just Christian ethic for refugee welcome need not look the same from place to place, so long as the needs that exist with greatest urgency, in closest proximity, are the needs being met, or at least addressed, by the local congregation.

---

18. Carens, *Immigrants and the Right to Stay*, 18–19.

Part 1: Arriving as an Undocumented Refugee

Exclusionary Walls—The Challenge of Communitarianism

Communitarian ethicists, by contrast to the cosmopolitans, argue that borders are morally required in order to ensure the security and welfare of the members of the political community residing within them. In order to maintain security, a community must be able to control access to its physical space. Thus, communitarians argue, nation-states should be able to restrict immigration, even to refugees. Michael Walzer, a leading proponent for the sovereign nation-state's right to control its borders by restricting access to refugees, argues in his book *Spheres of Justice* that the right to exclude migrants is an essential expression of the nation-state's right to self-determination. Sovereign self-determination includes a nation-state's desire to preserve a certain culture, population, resources, and above all, to protect its people.

Communitarians point out that accepting refugees into a sovereign state can change the balance of its internal status quo. If excessive numbers of new people are admitted as refugees, the enlarged population can pose a risk to the community's priority of security and welfare. When security is threatened, communitarians will argue for refusing entry, and this requires border controls. In our world of nation-states and bordered territories, every sovereign nation has established entrance policies towards migrants in order for the nation-state to maintain its culture, religion, and politics. Here lies the challenge for the refugee seeking a safe haven.

As will be discussed more fully in the next chapter on sovereignty and political theology, an important premise to accepting "refugee welcome" as a just immigration ethic is understanding that the need of the refugee and the purpose of the *polis* are the same: a stable community governed by the rule of law. Translating this goal into an ethical immigration entrance policy for refugees, Bretherton argues that:

> The just political judgment to be made in relation to refugees is at what point the inclusion of more refugees threatens to destabilize any given arena of law and order and not, as so many other responses to refugees suppose, the

point at which either territorial integrity, ethnic or cultural homogeneity, or economic power is threatened.[19]

Thus, there must be limits on how many refugees a nation-state can admit to its membership to maintain its stability. The rub comes in assessing where the admissions cutoff lies.

Christian ethicists who take the communitarian stance have far more nuanced arguments today that resonate with people's sense of societal belonging. Christian political and ethicist writers such as Mark Amstutz, Peter Meilaender, and Esther Reed have been able to acknowledge, and even affirm, the concerns of humanitarian cosmopolitans, and yet still support the sovereign rights, duties, and benefits of belonging to a bordered nation-state. This belonging, and protection, is after all, what the refugee is seeking as well when entering the US for asylum. More recent writers in the field are finding that the two paradigms are not mutually exclusive.

For example, Mark Amstutz, in his 2017 book *Just Immigration*, describes the two conflicting paradigms of cosmopolitanism and communitarianism and their necessary interrelation. He acknowledges that people are more important, morally, than nation-states, but that without the protections that nation-states provide, such "a claim is meaningless."[20] He gives weight to communitarian concerns of obedience to the law, the effects of immigration on a society's more vulnerable members, and the need for financial support from the nation-state for its infrastructure and for the indigent. But he recognizes the need for balance.

One of the concerns that congregants often express when faced with the question of welcoming the refugee into their communities is the fear of breaking the law while trying to love one's neighbor. For these congregants who privilege obedience to the law, the communitarian stance becomes even more attractive. Amstutz points out that the communitarian viewpoint supports a sense of security and belonging among members of a society. The nation-state supports human flourishing by providing a stable

19. Bretherton, "The Duty of Care," 49–50.
20. Amstutz, *Just Immigration*, 95.

Part 1: Arriving as an Undocumented Refugee

place in which to grow relationships with one another in social solidarity. A sense of belonging requires immediacy and concrete connection to specific others, not achievable within the ephemeral concept of a global community. Importantly, in addition to the shared social benefits of community and identity, there remains a basic human need for shelter and protection that the bordered state provides.

While acknowledging that *cosmopolitan* ideals influence and support most Christian advocacy groups on the question of immigration (the biblical foundation to "welcoming the stranger" cannot be ignored), Amstutz proposes several aspects of *communitarian* thinking that could strengthen a Christian approach to migration policy. Among these enhancements are the communitarian priorities of social solidarity and national sovereignty. Solidarity is a way of including others into the community. But, Amstutz cautions, there are negative aspects to growing community as well, including humanity's tendency towards conflict and competition.[21] For many, the objection to welcoming refugees relates to competition for jobs and social resources.

Communitarians consider that peaceful order is best preserved by having societal laws—and enforcing them. To offer a peaceful community to the refugee means that not all migrants can be received across US borders. Barring access preserves resources, but also creates conflict with citizens and others who object to immigration restraints. The discernment process may require compromise. Congregants may be asking themselves, "How can we preserve earthly peace, address pleas from refugees to access our community, and respect federal law limits on their entry?"

Orderliness and protection from harm are significant priorities of the communitarian model. Amstutz lifts up the work of another communitarian, Stephen Macedo, who argues that a moral approach to migration requires giving preference to the citizen over the alien, while government officials must devise policies that favor employment of low-income citizens ahead of entering

---

21. Amstutz, *Just Immigration*, 100.

The Morality of Border Walls and the New Cosmopolitanism

migrants.[22] Perhaps, like Carens, Amstutz and Macedo would support long-term, undocumented, resident aliens to be given a pathway to citizenship once inside the gates so that they could be more readily welcomed. There needs to be a middle ground. A just Christian immigration ethic must somehow combine a cosmopolitan emphasis on the human dignity of the refugee while supporting communitarian concepts of order and safety, including the "indispensable role of political community in advancing human well-being."[23]

Another communitarian proponent of border walls and the sense of security and solidarity they bring is Peter Meilaender (whose criticisms of Catholic Social Teaching and unbridled cosmopolitanism were shared earlier). Meilaender, like his contemporary Amstutz, concludes that there must be a sharing of interests, a middle ground between the cosmopolitan priorities of other ethicists and the communitarian view that he supports. In fact, he closes his book *Toward a Theory of Immigration*, by conceding that "if borders need not be completely open, neither should they be completely closed."[24]

Of interest here is the question Meilaender raises about prioritizing people and granting legal preferences for members of a political community or *polis*. Meilaender asks whether politically, we may, or even must, prefer our "own"—with the backing of sovereign power. And, in considering whether we can prefer our own, he asks *who* our own might be. He suggests they would be our family, friends, and neighbors—the proximate loved ones and others close at hand, those with a shared cultural identity or affinity—as making up our political community, and, thus, deserving preference.

Ironically, Meilaender's specific question for communitarians in assessing whom we should protect—"Who are our own?"—was answered differently by cosmopolitan Christian writer Justin Ashworth in his cosmopolitan-focused work discussed earlier. Ashworth answered that "our people" are "church people"—"God's

22. Amstutz, *Just Immigration*, 90–91.
23. Amstutz, *Just Immigration*, 109.
24. Meilaender, *Theory of Immigration*, 8.

Part 1: Arriving as an Undocumented Refugee

people"—giving a cosmopolitan answer to a communitarian question. Ashworth proposes that if we are to give preferences to a political community, as Meilaender suggests, then we must define our community as followers of Christ, through whom all are welcome, even nonbelievers, and thus all borders should be opened wide, and border walls no longer needed.[25]

A Reformed perspective on this view, which privileges the Christian community while opening it to all comers, evolves from Calvin's doctrine of election. In the Reformed view, God's eternal election in Jesus Christ initiates the whole process of salvation. Those who follow Christ have been elected to serve God in this world and receive the gift of election.[26] We cannot save ourselves, but God can, and does, save us through God's grace alone. In our contemporary context, this saving grace of Christ gives Christians the freedom to be involved in issues that have become concerns for the world: justice, peacemaking, and welcoming the refugee. In freedom, trusting in God, churches can act to offer hospitality to the refugee with love enough to spare.

We can also trust in Christ to welcome all who trust in him. As the Second Helvetic Confession of the Reformed tradition puts it:

> Let Christ therefore be the looking glass in whom we may contemplate our predestination. We shall have a sufficiently clear and sure testimony that we are inscribed in the Book of Life if we have fellowship in Christ, and he is ours and we are his in true faith.[27]

Putting our trust in Christ is a posture churches can take as a basis for refugee welcome. Knowing that we have been "elected" in Christ, we are free to extend a gracious welcome to the refugee, to help the other, and trust in God's benevolence towards us. Moreover, the resident refugees among us can also be understood as God's "elect." Calvin connected the perseverance of the persecuted refugee with the idea of predestination. "It is perseverance that maintained the

---

25. Ashworth, "Who Are Our People?," 496.
26. McKim, *Introducing the Reformed Faith*, 116–17.
27. Bullinger, "Second Helvetic Confession," 92.

The Morality of Border Walls and the New Cosmopolitanism

Huguenots in the time of their political disempowerment," Calvin wrote—a perseverance he attributed to their election.[28]

Welcoming Walls—The New Cosmopolitanism

A more nuanced form of cosmopolitanism encourages welcome while recognizing the benefits of protective walls and the orderly society that the bordered nation-state can provide. Similarly, a more open, nimble form of communitarianism provides greater latitude for opening border gates in order to welcome more refugees responsibly. This trend towards a middle ground is something theologian Esther Reed identifies as "Post-2001 New Cosmopolitanism,"[29] espoused by ethicists like Singer, promoting a broader understanding of the international impact of economic differences, climate change, and political actions that know no borders.

"Cosmopolitanisation . . . crosses frontiers like a stowaway,"[30] Reed muses. She explains this image as a new understanding about the connectedness of all people as the reason we should "reconceptualize our transnational interdependence."[31] In other words, our world is made up of bordered nation-states, but their borders cannot hold back the people looking for refuge, nor should they. The Reformed faith perspective aligns well with the "new cosmopolitanism" that both embraces all comers, while insisting on an ordered polity governed by the rule of law.

Churches and congregants might find this nuanced form of Christian cosmopolitanism to be the most palatable. The "new cosmopolitanism" acknowledges the reality of borders, while permitting space for welcome, and values a secure sense of social belonging that nation-states can provide the refugee. Adopting "borders that welcome" remind us that the true end of humanity is not for a protected society, but rather the possibility of human

---

28. Link, "Election and Predestination," 118.
29. Reed, *Theology for International Law*, 15.
30. As quoted in Reed, *Theology for International Law*, 15.
31. Reed, *Theology for International Law*, 15.

Part 1: Arriving as an Undocumented Refugee

flourishing in communion with God.[32] Resetting the ethical frame to this bigger picture presents borders that are no longer an obstacle in the path, but rather the "face we present to the world."[33] This new understanding of borders recognizes the sovereignty of the nation-state while offering a Christ-centered way of being and doing that treats the stranger with humanity and dignity.

This new cosmopolitanism approach to borders also lends itself to theological politics as a foundational part of a flourishing life. A flourishing life is not merely for the individual, but also for all society. Through our social connections, "flourishing emerges out of and depends on being embedded in some form of common life . . . as symbiotic with the flourishing of others."[34] With this goal in mind, a new Christian cosmopolitanism demands a relationship between the community behind the border walls and the strangers who presents themselves at the gate.

In order to open walls towards relationships, borders can be seen as a structural frame to "orientating a nation to the rest of the world in a way that presents an enquiring, confident, hospitable face."[35] This hybrid approach to understanding border walls respects both national borders and the needs of the refugee. Border walls as the "face" of a nation provides a less daunting entry point for the stranger and, instead, establishes a place where relationship, and welcome, can begin.

This new Christian cosmopolitan model of immigration ethics is the middle ground we need. It offers support for border controls to provide protection to those within the walls while encouraging policies of welcome and acceptance of the refugee outside them. This middle-ground approach stakes a more moderate position between the communitarian view supported by Mark Amstutz and Peter Meilaender, on the one hand, and the open-borders model of the more liberal brand of cosmopolitanism

---

32. Bretherton, "The End of National Borders," 7.
33. Bretherton, "The End of National Borders," 8.
34. Bretherton, *Christ and the Common Life*, 17–18.
35. Bretherton, *Christ and the Common Life*, 17–18.

The Morality of Border Walls and the New Cosmopolitanism

espoused by political theorist Peter Singer or even the vision of borderless states encouraged by ethicists Carens and Ashworth.

Where one lands on the question of "open borders" versus carefully "regulated borders," or more "porous borders" somewhere in the middle, may depend on who it is that is seeking border entry. All people are owed the dignity of respect and care as human beings in the process of applying for access to a neighboring nation-state. But both communitarian and cosmopolitan ethicists agree that when the person seeking entry into a host nation-state is a refugee, that person is owed a special duty of care.

Congregants and churches considering how and whether to welcome the refugee in their communities can now see that refugees are a special group of migrants in most urgent need of political asylum. Once undocumented refugees enter the bordered territory, then churches must decide how to respond. If our political theology is one of common flourishing, how should we treat the neighbor undocumented refugee family? Does their legal status, as either authorized or unauthorized aliens, make a difference to our welcome?

For many, legal status does matter. One of the challenges congregants continue to face in discerning their views about the morality of border walls is the legal status of the migrant crossing them. Even a refugee fleeing persecution is subject to suspicion and rejection the moment that person's status is declared to be "illegal."[36] In the view of political theologian Robert Heimburger, the "illegal alien" in America forms a vulnerable and exploited underclass in need of redeeming. As such, Heimburger argues for mercy.

Heimburger's conclusions about the plight of the undocumented alien living in the US for asylum are apt for our study. His first claim is that undocumented refugees lack advocates.

---

36. Social historian Mae Ngai argues that more restrictive immigration policies in the US created the "illegal alien" by limiting entry too severely. She describes the "illegal alien" as "*a new legal and political subject* whose inclusion within the nation was simultaneously a social reality and a legal impossibility . . . Such aliens in the U.S. are 'impossible subjects' as a people who cannot be and a problem that cannot be solved." Ngai, *Impossible Subjects*, 4–5 [emphasis in the original].

Part 1: Arriving as an Undocumented Refugee

Heimburger observed that in the 1960s, while legal rights for US citizens increased, the legislature and courts developed legal definitions and categories that classified the alien as subordinate to citizens, and thus with fewer rights.[37] Without advocates among legislators, the long-term undocumented residents of the US who are classified as "illegal aliens" are unable to curtail the government's efforts to limit their rights and even remove them from the country altogether.

Heimburger argues that "a Christian narrative of the healing of nations stands at odds with treating those from other nations like aliens."[38] Instead, he sees theological understandings of far-flung peoples as opportunities for neighbors to draw near to one another, to be made complete in the people of God, and to be the church. Thus, he proposes possible ethical courses of action that reconnect nation with neighbor, and human with human.

Among his recommendations, Heimburger suggests a new understanding of the purpose of border walls in terms of the activity of guarding.[39] Heimburger focuses on the guarding of places as a human activity under God's ultimate care[40]—to be carried out under God's direction of fairness—and for God to judge the guardians and "those under their care, including migrants."[41]

Taking lessons from the communitarian perspective, Heimburger recommends that when there is an influx of refugees, nation-states should set entrance policies that protect the common good of the community within the nation-state. He concludes that a just Christian ethic of immigration requires a just entrance policy at the border that "fends off threats of harm to what a society shares."[42] Thus, it is not open borders that are required, but rather setting a fair basis by which to exclude or limit access to the *polis* that the border guardians protect.

37. Heimburger, *God and the Illegal Alien*, 210.
38. Heimburger, *God and the Illegal Alien*, 210–11.
39. Heimburger, *God and the Illegal Alien*, 95, 103–4.
40. Heimburger, *God and the Illegal Alien*, 104–6.
41. Heimburger, *God and the Illegal Alien*, 211.
42. Heimburger, *God and the Illegal Alien*, 211.

Heimburger's second helpful finding relates to remedies. When assessing the situation of the resident alien refugee who has settled without authorization within the US, Heimburger urges a more proportional assessment of the wrong committed and the remedy imposed. It is the nation-state that imposes the law against entry and residence without a visa as being illegal. Residing within the territory without authorization is, thus, not a wrong in itself (*malum in se*) but rather is wrong because it has been declared prohibited (*mala prohibita*).[43] As a result, the punishment for that wrong should not exceed the wrong carried out.

In other words, Heimburger's analysis of US immigration policy through a Christian lens is leading us to a place of greater mercy, and proportionality, in the remedies brought against the undocumented refugee. Staying within the Christian tradition, Heimburger recasts immigration enforcement as an opportunity for ministry, where our sovereign God, not the nation-state, calls us to protect human life.[44]

What this ministry would look like in terms of the *polis* might be lobbying for legislative change for amnesty to be granted to long-term resident alien refugees who have settled in the US, held a job, paid taxes, and done everything possible to live as a full citizen, but merely lack citizenship status. It might be regularization of Mexican nationals who come to the US as manual workers, granting them visa status to come and go with the seasons, so that they can maintain their family ties in Mexico. A ministry of advocating for the undocumented refugee in the *polis* might also look like judicial reform, where judges are encouraged to consider the impact that removal or detention has on the undocumented refugee resident alien's family, workplace, and community within the US.

The way forward is for churches and congregations to navigate. I encourage them to take the middle-ground approach of the "new cosmopolitanism" where the rule of law matters, but so does compassion for the persecuted stranger in need. Combining

---

43. Heimburger, *God and the Illegal Alien*, 135.
44. Heimburger, *God and the Illegal Alien*, 211.

Part 1: Arriving as an Undocumented Refugee

themes of social justice and mercy could lead to changes in the US government's approach to undocumented resident aliens in the US and encourage congregations to be more proactive in getting to know their neighbors. But even as denominational leadership calls for faithful witness and legal reform, too many Christians remain silent.

Heimburger and others recognize that "many laypeople are a step behind"[45] on embracing refugee welcome, especially for undocumented refugees. He observes that "Christians in the United States fail to reflect on the witness of the Christian tradition on migration, holding to a law-and-order response to illegal immigration."[46] But even an ordered society allows room for compassion. Perhaps there is room for both justice and mercy. Before we close our borders and condemn the illegal act of unauthorized entry, we have an ethical obligation as Christians to consider the safety of the refugee—and our moral duty to assist that person as our neighbor in need.

---

45. Heimburger, *God and the Illegal Alien*, 215.
46. Heimburger, *God and the Illegal Alien*, 215.

Chapter 2

Bare Life and the Reformed Faith Perspective on Refugees

"When an alien resides with you in your land, you shall not oppress the alien."

—Lev 19:33 (NRSV)

BARE LIFE AND BEYOND

While assessing the morality of border walls, it is easy to lose sight of the human dimension of the refugees who seek asylum behind those walls—whether they be people seeking permission to enter or those applying for asylum once inside. It is essential to see the refugee as a person, as God's creation, and also as one dispossessed of a *polis*, stripped of the political identity that comes with having a homeland. Such individuals denuded of rights and protections have been described by political philosophers as "bare life." Living as bare life are human beings without voice or vote, rights or recognition.

How we understand the individual refugee in relationship to human rights and political rights will determine our views on how to welcome and advocate for our undocumented neighbor. It will also inform the way we consider the plight of refugee families separated at borders, the arrest and removal of undocumented refugees residing in the US, and the ways we might welcome undocumented refugees if they showed up in our churches or moved into the house next door.

Bare Life: A Broken Human-Citizen Link

Political philosophers like Hannah Arendt and Giorgio Agamben, as well as Christian ethicist Luke Bretherton, warn that when the refugee is stripped of political identity and reduced to bare life, that person's chance for survival is weakened by being relegated to an existence outside the political life of the nation-state. "Bare life" is merest natural life, the state of being born and existing without political status as citizen or subject.

In his book *Homo Sacer*, Giorgio Agamben describes "bare life" as the natural life that comes with birth, sacred life in the eyes of God, yet, in extreme totalitarian political systems, a life capable of being killed by the nation-state without being declared a homicide.[1] It is bare, natural life to which rights and political belonging can attach, but if they do not, the body becomes an outcast, a "person without a nation," a problem to be resolved.[2] This is the life experience faced by stateless refugees outside the border wall. Reconciling what Agamben calls the "birth-nation" and "[human]-citizen" link with the "bare life" of the refugee, we can begin to build a Christian political ethic that restores human rights to the refugee within a sovereign political duty of care. In an interesting examination of "biopolitics" and the role of the refugee,

1. Agamben, *Homo Sacer*, 82–83.
2. Agamben, *Homo Sacer*, 131.

Bare Life and the Reformed Faith Perspective on Refugees

Agamben sees the refugee as forcing a crisis in the political order by the very fact of not fitting in.

Agamben makes his argument by tracing the historical development of human rights in relation to the growth of the sovereign state. He begins with the paradox that Hannah Arendt reveals at the close of her book *Origins of Totalitarianism:* that the refugee, who "should have embodied the rights of man par excellence ... signals instead the concept's radical crisis."[3] Agamben argues persuasively from this launching point that whenever humanity's natural rights are linked to the system of the nation-state, they are ultimately lost forever. When citizens flee from their homeland, or are cut off from connection there, they no longer count as citizens within its borders. Instead of representing humanity with the fullness of human rights, they represent statelessness and have lost all rights completely.

Here is the fine line between bare life and citizenship. The individual becomes a citizen through birth in a nation-state. Once a citizen repudiates his sovereign nation, seeking protection elsewhere as a refugee, he breaks the connection between nativity and nationality—the human/citizen link—and loses his political rights. The refugee, outside the connection to and protection of a *polis,* is relegated to bare life, with no rights; and no nation is obligated to provide protection or care. It would then seem that only ethical concerns raised by others on the refugee's behalf could motivate a nation-state's voluntary willingness to intercede politically for the refugee by offering asylum.

In order to redress the political problem of the refugee in crisis, Agamben argues that the "concept of the refugee"—and the life it represents—must be recognized apart from the rigid dichotomy of citizen–*polis*/bare life–lawless.[4] Only by reconstructing international political relations to include bare life within political life can the refugee find a place at the table—within the sphere of the sovereign duty of care and within a concept of human rights. Applying these ideas to the modern challenge of refugee welcome

3. As quoted in Agamben, *Homo Sacer,* 126.
4. Agamben, *Homo Sacer,* 134.

Part 1: Arriving as an Undocumented Refugee

requires congregants to accept the political as a place of meaning and conversation for their church community and worship life. Without political support, bare life cannot survive.

Bare Life: A Broken Humanitarian-Political Link

Once we recognize the helpless position of bare life in political society, we need to fashion an appropriate response. And it must be a political one. The intentional separation of political and humanitarian assistance has proved to be shortsighted for not addressing the underlying causes of refugee flight. In today's complex world, we need to reconnect the decoupling of political and humanitarian responses to the refugee crisis through political theology. As we learned above, refugees need what the healthy *polis* provides: protective laws and a place for peaceful existence. Refugees need sovereign protections from the life-threatening persecution of the homeland they fled.

Yet the political problem persists. Illustrating how the political isolation of the refugee has become systematized in our humanitarian relief efforts, Bretherton describes how the charter obligation of the office of the United Nations High Commissioner for Refugees is exclusively humanitarian and social—not political. As a result, instead of providing advocacy for legal rights and recognition of the refugee, humanitarian aid organizations such as the United Nations focus exclusively on bare life survival needs while maintaining "a secret solidarity with the very powers they ought to fight."[5] In a glaring example of what stripping political protections from humanitarian aid looks like, Bretherton points out the refusal of the Red Cross International Committee to speak out against the actions of the Nazis during World War II on grounds of avowed political neutrality, despite having knowledge of the Nazi concentration camps.[6]

---

5. Agamben, *Homo Sacer*, 88–90.
6. Bretherton, *Christianity and Contemporary Politics*, 141.

To avoid repeating the same mistakes, churches and congregants must be willing to see political recognition of everyone living in their community as one aspect of the aid required by the refugee. By these lights, the most pressing need of the refugee is political, and requires a polity with a stable rule of law, rather than humanitarian aid. Although addressing creature care needs is essential for survival and is the appropriate response to the crisis of natural disasters and displacements caused by war, humanitarian aid is only ever a temporary and incomplete response to the underlying political problem facing the refugee.

Thus, for churches to assist the undocumented refugee, they will need to identify an underlying political theology. One part of a political response to refugee welcome is to give a voice to the refugee through offering political standing, or at the very least advocacy. To hive off the political from the humanitarian leaves the perverse result of further marginalizing the refugee as bare life and leaving that isolated person outside the rule of law, or worse, criminalized as an outlaw. Instead, by offering welcome, churches can help redeem the bare life of the refugee by offering community belonging, advocacy, and a place of standing in the *polis*, a seat at the neighborhood table.

Redemptive Responses for Integrating the Refugee into Political Life

Joining a church-based conversation about returning the refugee to a life that is both political and humane may present challenges for those congregants who have always lamented hearing what they call "politics" from the pulpit. But political theology represents a Christ-centered call for human flourishing of everyone in the *polis*. Our Christian life together is necessarily political, although it is a different kind of politics from the acrimony of partisan feuding across political party lines. Taking the *polis* and the refugee seriously, we can begin to educate ourselves about the laws and protections our country provides to refugees and the undocumented

Part 1: Arriving as an Undocumented Refugee

asylum-seeker. We can begin to see our neighbor refugees as human beings with a name and a face, an identity and a story.

When we connect with the asylum-seekers whom we meet living in our communities, we begin to be in relationship with that person, and soon recognize the gift that they bring to our lives. Created in God's image, loved by God as we are, the refugee, even if an unauthorized one, provides the face of the other, at the same time as the face in which we might see the reflection of Christ.

In living a life of Christian discipleship, churches and congregants can experience a profoundly deeper faith experience in welcoming the refugees who seek entry into the community, regardless of their legal status. Welcome invariably involves personal contact which easily blossoms into friendship. As Anglican theologian Samuel Wells comments, fellowship with the refugee is a starting place. Sharing food and offering friendship with a stranger, he argues, are gestures based on trust that the person befriended is a precious creation. Yet, he admits that the stranger is a "gift that is slow to reveal and hard to receive."[7] On an interpersonal level, just as the Good Samaritan provided personal connection and merciful assistance to a neighbor in need, we can find welcome in our hearts when we begin to see the refugee not as anonymous bare life, but as a person who is a gift and a blessing for our lives as well.

The Reformed Faith Perspective on Refugee Welcome in the *Polis*

For churches and their congregants in the Presbyterian-Reformed tradition grappling with undocumented refugee welcome, it may be helpful to remember that the Reformed tradition traces its roots back to the sixteenth-century Protestant reforms of John Calvin. Calvin was a French humanist, raised in the Roman Catholic Church, trained as a lawyer, and committed to the religious reform already underway in Western Europe. His early activism in the reform movement of the church led to his close escape from arrest

---

7. Wells, *God's Companions*, 107.

Bare Life and the Reformed Faith Perspective on Refugees

by Roman Church authorities while he was a law student in Paris, France, in 1534. He fled to the Protestant territory of Switzerland, arriving in Geneva as a refugee at the age of twenty-six. There he found safety, protection, and the freedom to worship God as a Christian without interference from Rome. He made Switzerland his permanent home and became a leading reformer of the church as well as a highly influential leader in the political life of the city of Geneva.

Calvin's own refugee status led him to aid other refugees who arrived in Geneva during his thirty years of asylum there. From 1536 to 1564, the population of Geneva nearly doubled to 21,000 inhabitants. Over 10,000 of the newcomers were adult male refugees, and with them came uncounted numbers of women and children.[8] What Calvin lived and learned as a refugee in Geneva influenced how he understood God's providential care of God's creation and God's freedom to grant grace. Calvin's understanding of the doctrine of providence provided the Reformed tradition a picture "of God's continuing, intimate care both of all human life, and of all creation."[9] Calvin also saw a scriptural mandate in aiding the stranger and in trusting God's presence among the exiled. Calvin's call for compassionate care for the refugee was also motivated by gratitude to God—a Reformed faith tenet, but also Calvin's grateful personal response to God for his own providential rescue.[10]

John Calvin's experience of being a refugee fleeing religious persecution had a lasting influence on his theology and pastoral ministry. Although he did not write about his personal life in any detail, he was marked by his experience of life-threatening persecution and the consequences of living in exile. These experiences led him closer to God and a recognition of God "as the first refugee, trekking with the people of Israel through the desert."[11] In Geneva, Calvin admitted how "it is very hard to have to live far from

---

8. Benedict, "Calvin and the Transformation of Geneva," 11.
9. Zachman, "John Calvin," 147.
10. Engammare, "Une Certaine Idée," 17.
11. Oberman, *Initia Calvini*, 153.

Part 1: Arriving as an Undocumented Refugee

one's homeland."[12] He identified on a personal level with the exiled. He wrote in the preface to his book of lessons on Daniel that his personal experience of being a refugee himself is what drove him to "publicly rescue and help the French" in Geneva, drawing parallels between the French refugees and the exiled Israelites.[13]

Theologian Ruben Rosario Rodriguez describes John Calvin's reforms in Geneva as extending beyond the church to the governance of the community at large, including its establishment of hospitals[14] for the welfare of the people, an academy for excellence in education, and a center for mission work. Calvin built a system of social welfare in the city and contributed to a benevolence fund to support the refugees flocking to Geneva from all over Europe. He organized the Presbyterian-Reformed church structure led by church "elders" in a "consistory" board to govern the congregation and created a "diaconate" of congregants to share in a ministry of compassion.[15] His congregation cared for all Genevans, not merely church members. And the foundation for his church structure was entirely scriptural.

Calvin influenced the reform of Geneva through consistent preaching, direction given to the shared governance of the church consistory, and the application of civil law (his legal background made him an invaluable advisor to municipal authorities as well as church leaders).[16] Calvin transformed both the ecclesial and civil society in Geneva—while taking care of thousands of refugees. Moreover, Calvin believed that civil magistrates were God's lieutenants on earth, with an obligation to defend the true religion.[17] Thus, he had no hesitation to implement church ethics, including refugee welcome, through civil laws, despite recognizing the unique and separate spheres of each.

12. Oberman, "*Initia Calvini*," 154.
13. Engammare, "Une Certaine Idée," 19.
14. Rosario Rodríguez, "Calvin's Legacy of Compassion," 44–62, 51.
15. Rosario Rodríguez, "Calvin's Legacy of Compassion," 53–54.
16. Benedict, "Calvin and the Transformation of Geneva," 5–7.
17. Benedict, "Calvin and the Transformation of Geneva," 7.

Bare Life and the Reformed Faith Perspective on Refugees

Providing compassion and support to people in need, as Calvin did, through both church and *polis*, based on theological underpinnings of God's providence and scriptural authority, is one aspect of a Reformed approach to the refugee residing in our midst. It finds its expression in "neighborliness" today. Neighborliness is a grassroots remedy to democratic political outcomes that have become skewed by the rule of the many overlooking the needs of the few.

Applying the theological concern to care for the "other," both through church and in our shared political life together, we can remedy political injustice through personal and community relationships with the undocumented refugee. In this way, refugee welcome rightly boils down to relationship-building. And relationships are always contextual. Being a good neighbor also "necessitates good judgments about how to embody justice and love with *this* person or *these* people in *this* place, at *this* time."[18] There is no one size of neighborliness that fits all communities or congregations. The challenge for churches is to forge the best path for refugee welcome in their own context.

Christian immigration ethics help us to frame a way of thinking about the refugee and points towards privileging the refugee's need for access to a peaceful polity bound by the rule of law. Understanding border walls as a place of interface for refugee welcome, and bordered territory as a needful measure to maintain a peaceful *polis*, churches and congregants can begin to think of ways to welcome the neighbor refugee by meeting them where they are.

Welcoming the politically stateless refugee across borders is grounded in the same ethical arguments as one would welcome the asylum-seeker already resident without authorization in the United States. The long-term resident refugee can be welcomed under the new cosmopolitan ethic of balanced equities. But once resident inside the US, undocumented refugees face the problem of sovereignty and the law—under both the laws of the

---

18. Bretherton, *Christianity and Contemporary Politics*, 45 (emphasis in the original).

Part 1: Arriving as an Undocumented Refugee

nation-state and the laws of God. We turn to these topics in the chapters that follow.

SUMMARY OF PART 1

Part 1 described the spectrum of ethical approaches concerning international migration across the borders of nation-states, from open borders to closed border walls. It found that political theologians and Christian ethicists are converging on an ethical middle ground for refugee welcome across the borders of nation-states. This midpoint ethic is the new cosmopolitanism. It tolerates borders, but encourages a special duty of care towards, and access rights for, refugees. Adopting this new cosmopolitanism approach, churches and congregants can agree that border walls are needful but should serve as an interface where the refugee can be met and welcomed as an expression of God's redeeming love and as a show of human dignity.

Part 1 also gave background on the Reformed tradition's understanding of God's intended relationships for God's people with the refugee to be merciful and welcoming. Historically, refugee welcome has been part of the Reformed faith's practical theology since the time of its founding by pastor-theologian John Calvin, himself a religious refugee. Inspired by Scripture and personal experience, Calvin became a leader in welcoming the other religious refugees that fled to his place of refuge in Geneva. Providing a model for us to follow today, Calvin found God's providential plan for creation to include stable human communities, places for peaceful society, and protection and respect for the rule of law.

These learnings are important for they allow churches and congregants to take the next step in their discernment about refugee welcome in their own neighborhoods. In embracing a nuanced new cosmopolitanism, and the dignity of human life, we can now proceed from accepting the moral needfulness of welcoming the undocumented refugee, to understanding the legal impediments to doing so and the challenge those impediments present to the church.

Part 2

Residing as an Undocumented Refugee

Chapter 3

State Sovereignty and the Rights of the Resident Alien

"The alien who resides with you shall be to
you as the citizen among you; you shall love
the alien as yourself, for you were aliens in the
land of Egypt: I am the LORD your God."

— LEV 19:34 (NRSV)

INTRODUCTION

HAVING ESTABLISHED THE ETHICAL justification for welcoming the refugee into the *polis* under a more nuanced form of cosmopolitanism, I now address the legal impediments towards refugee welcome and the countervailing Christian imperatives for welcoming. I begin by looking at the treatment and life experience of the undocumented refugee in the US, and the conflicted perception of the undocumented refugee who is present in society without legal

Part 2: Residing as an Undocumented Refugee

authorization, on the one hand, and as a beloved creature of God, on the other.

To help congregants and churches discern what ethical action to take regarding the long-term resident undocumented refugee, I examine both the sovereignty claims of the nation-state and the sovereignty of God. I describe the Reformed theological understanding of civil laws and political life working together as part of God's gift for our lives in an ordered Christian society. I also employ an Augustinian framework for understanding the sovereignty of God in contrast to the sovereignty of the nation-state.

Historically, I consider further the life of Reformer John Calvin as a refugee, and the influence his migrant experience had on his expression of scriptural interpretation and theological doctrine as informative for church and congregational discernment about refugee welcome today. I conclude with a look at the "ordering of loves" in Christian theology as loving our neighbors, be they far or near, as expressed by Reformed theologian Karl Barth. The notion of loving our proximate neighbor then provides the basis for a practical theology of welcoming the long-term resident refugee in our own neighborhoods, regardless of the refugee's legal status.

Organizing the Inquiry around the Sacred and Secular

In equipping congregations to take a moral view on how to interact with the undocumented refugee living in America, politically and socially, I introduce terms and concepts in both law and theology. The information I provide lines up neatly between two worlds: the sacred and the secular. Our challenge as Christians is to find ways to live out the divine laws of the sacred in our secular world. Thus, to present the dichotomy, I organize scholarly material around laws, rights, and duties of the nation-state and then turn to theological reflection and a discussion of God's sovereignty over all creation, including nation-states.

Organized in this way, this second part of the book tracks our two lines of inquiry regarding the undocumented resident alien refugee: first, what do the laws of the US government permit for this group of people, and for our welcome of them? And second, as followers of Christ, what should our behavior be towards undocumented refugees? In the process, we will begin to see the possibility that not only are we, individually, called to love our neighbor, but also, the nation-states, as civil societies, are too.

Competing Allegiances

How sovereign America treats the unauthorized resident alien within its territory depends on US immigration and alienage laws, the applicability of protections under the US Constitution to noncitizen residents, and sovereign claims over the continuing control of migrants who have entered the country. For many Christians, how they treat the unauthorized resident alien within their communities depends on their discernment of scriptural teachings and the leading of the Spirit—independent of federal laws. In the Reformed tradition, however, there is a sense of unity between the workings of civil government and the life of the church.

Under the doctrine of covenant with God, Reformed theologians recognize the concept of humanity's freedom to join in communion with God and the freedom of the church to be in relationship with all God's creation. The church is free to witness Christ's gospel message of justice, love, and peace to the nation-state. The church proclaims its purpose and calling freely in the nation-state. And the nation-state is free to pursue its true calling: the pursuit of peace and justice.

Reformed theologian Karl Barth develops the idea of a "just" nation-state, and an "unjust" one. He acknowledges the church community's respect for just laws that uphold human dignity. By contrast, he describes the "unjust" state as having a "demonic quality" that "denies the church's witness, and demands its citizens to worship the state as they would God."[1] Recall that Barth lived and taught in Nazi Germany, where totalitarianism reigned, but he eventually fled to Switzerland for safety. He had witnessed firsthand

---

1. Barth, *Community*, 34.

Part 2: Residing as an Undocumented Refugee

the Nazi party's ideological invasion and corruption of the German Church, turning a religious institution into a political puppet.

Barth maintains the church has a priestly function with regard to the nation-state. The church must function to remind civil authorities of their responsibilities to treat humanity with dignity and respect. But he cautions that an "idolatrous" church would seek instead to become the nation-state, replacing its duty to preach, teach, and serve sacraments with the temptation for political power.[2] Instead, a church must work, pray, and struggle to maintain a just nation-state that seeks to maintain an earthly peace. By witnessing to Christ's teachings and reminding the nation-state of its political function, the church becomes more aware of its own political task. And, by extension, it becomes "impossible," Barth claims, "for the Christian to adopt an attitude of complete indifference to politics."[3]

John Calvin, Barth's predecessor by 400 years in Reformation Switzerland, also insisted that civil law was a necessity for a Christian society "because law and political government are the gift of God to man."[4] Civil law is a gift for teaching right behavior to help preserve earthly peace, rather than imposing harsh edicts or burdens. In his commentary on Exodus 18:13–25, Calvin describes political government as "the establishment of God's tribunal on earth by which God exercises the judges' office."[5] By extension, Calvin concludes, human political authority is derived from God as a means of limiting and guiding human behavior, rather than law and political governance being an instrument of authoritarian rule.

Calvin considered the nation-state to be God's creation and "absolutely necessary" to human existence because it permits the peaceful enjoyment of life in society, the worship of God, and reconciliation with one another.[6] Thus, the Reformed ethical outlook is centered on Christ and God's sovereign place over all creation,

2. Barth, *Community,* 132, 146–47.
3. Barth, *Community,* 162.
4. Reid, "John Calvin," 63.
5. Reid, "John Calvin," 63.
6. Reid, "John Calvin," 63.

State Sovereignty and the Rights of the Resident Alien

including the nation-states, in order that the church and civil society would remain in coexistence with, and accountable to, the Lordship of Jesus Christ and the kingdom of God.

Centuries later, still true to the Reformed tradition, Karl Barth's work on the role of civil authority is also based in Scripture. Barth looks at the Gospel of John and the relationship of Pilate to Jesus. He makes an elegant case that even Pilate, in failing justice by permitting the crucifixion of Jesus, served God's purposes by placing the civil authorities under God's redemption.[7] The relationship of God to sinners is no different from God's relationship to the powers of the nation-state, Barth concludes. Both sinful people and nation-states need redeeming and both are "within the Christological sphere."[8]

Furthering this theme of nation-state accountability to Christ, Christian ethicist Esther Reed reminds us that in the Christian tradition, the nations are ultimately answerable to God, with Christ as the eschatological judge.[9] Citing a passage from Matthew's Gospel, better known for its reminder to feed the hungry, give drink to the thirsty, and welcome the stranger, Reed reminds us that the gospel witness begins with a glimpse of the final judgment day.

> When the Son of Man comes in his glory, and all the angels with him, then he will sit on the throne of his glory. All the nations will be gathered before him, and he will separate people one from another as a shepherd separates the sheep from the goats . . .[10]

Scripture suggests that not only will people be judged at the end of times; but also, the nation-states themselves will be assessed based on their reception of the gospel of Jesus Christ and their faithfulness to the rule of God's law. And while the American nation-state is a secular one, congregant citizens of it can influence national policy and advocate for changes to legislation that would bring the

---

7. Barth, *Community*, 112–13.
8. Barth, *Community*, 120.
9. Reed, *Theology for International Law*, 21–22.
10. Matt 25:31–32 (NRSV).

Part 2: Residing as an Undocumented Refugee

exercise of sovereign rights closer in line with an ethic of Christian compassion for the refugee neighbor in need of welcome.

Yet living out our role as Christian neighbor to the resident alien refugee, whether documented or not, may lead us to cross-purposes with the federal government's position on removal of undocumented immigrants. How we reconcile our rights and obligations as US citizens of the nation-state and our faith commitments as disciples of Christ is the challenge we face as Christians. It explains why many churches find themselves at odds with the government over the treatment of undocumented resident aliens in the United States today.

Many law-abiding congregants who see God's creative work in the existence of the nation-state find it difficult to adopt a stance of opposition to civil laws—even if they may wish to express compassion for the refugee. How do church members reconcile these sometimes conflicted, yet Christ-centered, views concerning their shared society, one that includes long-term resident undocumented refugees? Both Calvin and Barth would encourage congregants to engage in their role as political Christians—equipped and empowered to think for themselves, as ethicists poised for action. Barth's essays in *Community, State, and Church* provide some helpful learning on how to manage respect for civil authority, and the obligation to agitate for a just state, as members of Christ's church under the sovereignty of God.

From there, another important part of the discernment process on refugee welcome is to learn what laws apply to asylum-seeking unauthorized resident refugees and to advocate for change where the laws are unjust or inequitably applied. Lack of understanding, or simply failing to inquire about the ethical dimension of undocumented refugee reception in America, is what leaves many mainline Protestants lethargic about the role they can play and what actions to take in the welcome of refugees into their home communities. To help educate our congregations about the applicable federal laws and God's sovereign law concerning refugee welcome, it is necessary to delve deeper into each.

State Sovereignty and the Rights of the Resident Alien

IN THE "EARTHLY CITY": ALIENS, REFUGEES, AND THE SOVEREIGNTY OF THE NATION-STATE

Aliens

Any asylum-seeker entering the US, or any other immigrant who settles in America, is described as an "alien" until that person acquires US citizenship. Refugees who have been granted asylum status are given legal permission to reside in the US and are included in the legal category of "resident alien." For those refugees who have been denied asylum permission to reside in the US, or any other immigrant who is in the US unlawfully, US law describes them as "aliens who are unlawfully present in the US,"[11] or more simply "undocumented."

The fact of the undocumented refugee's residence in the US is significant because it suggests the refugee has already established a place in the economic infrastructure of the community even if not provided with social benefits and rights afforded to authorized resident aliens and citizens. Under current US immigration laws, there is no means of rectifying an undocumented resident alien's illegal immigration status. There is no paper to file or plea to be made—without leaving the country first.

To make matters worse for the undocumented refugees trying to rectify their status, under the Illegal Immigration Reform and Immigrant Responsibility Act of 1996,[12] undocumented asylum-seekers residing in the US for over one year without filing for asylum, who are detained by immigration authorities and deported, or who leave the US for any reason and attempt to reenter, will be barred from reentry into the US for a ten-year period. This measure places undocumented asylum-seekers in the impossible situation of facing either dangerous living conditions in their home nation if they return there, or existence as an undocumented alien in the US with limited rights if they remain. It renders the

---

11. Heimburger, *God and the Illegal Alien*, 69.
12. U.S. House, "Illegal Immigration Reform Act."

Part 2: Residing as an Undocumented Refugee

undocumented resident refugee to a life lived under the constant fear of arrest and removal by immigration enforcement police.

Legal scholar Linda Bosniak articulates the unique problem facing the alien in America in her work *The Citizen and the Alien*. She recognizes that most nation-states reserve the broadest range of services and civil rights to its citizens. Those who lack citizenship status are designated as "aliens" and are denied the full extent of these societal benefits. When alienage in the US is long-term, or even permanent, aliens develop into a second-class caste in American society. Over time, their subordinate status to citizens seems misplaced when aliens pay taxes, abide by local laws, and contribute to society through their employment and service, just as do US citizens.

In the US, the law has been ambivalent about alienage as to rights and benefits. US alienage laws provide less favorable treatment for aliens than for citizens, but at the same time offer aliens some basic constitutional rights—such as due process (the right to trial and a bail hearing upon arrest) and nondiscrimination. Thus, being perceived as an alien in the US is a step up from bare life. The very classification as an "alien" designates political status. And it amplifies the nation-state's sovereign ability to set and maintain boundaries against outsiders, even when they are living inside its bordered walls.[13]

Bosniak addresses the question of what impact immigration law—how the nation-state can control its borders and who it allows to enter them—should have on alienage law, which covers noncitizens residing in national territory and participating in national life. Immigration law and alienage law are often in tension, especially regarding the removal of undocumented resident aliens who have been living in the US for extended periods of time.

Bosniak argues that alienage is a hybrid legal status category that lies at the nexus of the legal and moral worlds.

> On the one hand, it lies within the world of borders, sovereignty, and national community membership. This is the world of the government's immigration power, which

13. Bosniak, *The Citizen and the Alien*, 37.

State Sovereignty and the Rights of the Resident Alien

regulates decisions about the admission and exclusion of outsiders, and places conditions on their entry and residence. The very existence of alienage is a product of this world because the government designates aliens as such in the course of exercising its immigration power. In the broader landscape of American public law, this power remains exceptionally unconstrained. Yet alienage is also a social category that lies in the world of social relationships among territorially present persons. In this world, government power to impose disabilities on people based on their status is substantially constrained.[14]

It is this conflict whose ragged edge has cut across partisan political debates and disrupted the lives of many long-term resident undocumented aliens in America. It emanates from a tenacious holdover of claims under immigration laws against individual immigrants whom border patrol agents seek to capture and deport for having defied US entrance policies, even decades after their entry into America.

The conflict between immigration law and alienage law emerges when national concerns about membership rights attempt to strip aliens of their personhood rights, despite there being a limited number of constitutional guarantees[15] that apply to all persons in the US, aliens and citizens alike. At the very least, the

---

14. Bosniak, *The Citizen and the Alien*, 38.

15. The US Supreme Court has suggested in *dicta* that there is an open question as to the availability of Fourth Amendment rights (prohibition of unreasonable searches and seizures without a warrant) to resident aliens. See *United States v. Verdugo-Urquidez*, 494 U.S. 259, 272. More than a century ago, the Supreme Court established that the Fifth (due process) and Sixth (speedy trial and assistance of counsel in defense) Amendments apply to aliens in *Wong Wing v. U.S.*, 163 U.S. 228, 238 (1896). A decade earlier, *Yick Wo v. Hopkins, 118 U.S. 356 (1886)* established that the equal protection clause, based on a race claim, applies to aliens. More recently, in *Plyler v. Doe*, 457 U.S. 202, 215 (1982), the Supreme Court unanimously granted Fourteenth Amendment rights (equal protection) to resident aliens as "persons" under that clause—and carved out for all aliens a "zone of protected personhood" where the nation-state's membership control rights are "of no consequence at all." Bosniak, *The Citizen and the Alien*, 64.

Part 2: Residing as an Undocumented Refugee

legal acknowledgment of "personhood" grants the refugee a certain legitimacy—a step above statelessness, and more than "bare life."

The resulting mismatch of immigration and alienage laws is what Bosniak describes as a "jurisdictional dispute,"[16] but one with real impact on the lives of undocumented resident aliens, leaving them vulnerable and feeling unsafe in the very place where they came for refuge. Ultimately, the dispute is one over state powers and individual rights. Is the nation-state's discriminatory action against resident alien undocumented refugees a *legitimate* action under the government's *sovereign power* to regulate membership, or is it an *illegitimate* violation of the resident alien's *rights as a person*? Like so many legal debates, the outcome will depend on context. But for congregants, it is helpful to understand the unsettled state of the law.[17] Another factor for discernment is balancing the competing, and legitimate, concerns of preserving sovereign control, on the one hand, and personhood rights of the alien, on the other. Even as we follow US law and policy developments, every congregant must also make compassionate and nuanced decisions about neighbor love and refugee welcome, and how to apply it, in their towns and neighborhoods.

Undocumented Resident Alien Refugees as "Metic" Bare Life

In measuring how far sovereigns may legally discriminate against aliens for legitimate membership controls before it must give way to the equality of personhood, Bosniak inadvertently stumbles upon the "bare life" denigration of the status-less refugee. She

---

16. Bosniak, *The Citizen and the Alien*, 40.

17. Bosniak might push back against this description of competing claims as "unsettled law" as she does find some clear conclusions in case law history. She writes: "In sum, *Wing Wong, Yick Wo*, and more recently *Plyler*, stand for the proposition that when it comes to the alien's relationship with the government, the government's immigration power does not occupy the entire terrain. While non-citizens, by virtue of their alienage, are subject to the government's membership-regulating powers, they also inhabit a sphere of territorial personhood that remains insulated from the action of membership principles." Bosniak, *The Citizen and the Alien*, 55.

State Sovereignty and the Rights of the Resident Alien

finds her way here by analyzing US alienage laws through the lens of Michael Walzer's landmark study of community membership in *Spheres of Justice*. Walzer considers a nation-state's "admissions policy" to its bordered territory using the rubric of "membership." Each sphere, or category, of sovereign life involves aspects of its governing power. Membership is one such sphere. In analyzing the status of immigrants residing in a democratic national community and identifying their membership category, Walzer provides a framework for legal scholars like Bosniak, and Christian ethicists like us, to think about the US legal approach to alienage rights.

Walzer's membership sphere concept has been widely used by immigration ethicists to support the proposal that the nation-state is a membership community and is justified in shutting out any outsiders from entry. The nation-state membership community holds shared meanings, a unique culture, and a way of life, which it preserves for its members. Walzer bases this claim of a members-only nation-state on a theory of "distributive justice," arguing that the nation-state distributes membership as a primary good. He views sovereign control over admissions to the membership community as a significant value, perhaps the preeminent one, of the nation-state.[18] Yet, he, too, recognizes that there are moral dimensions to membership entry that can compel the granting of admission to certain individuals or groups, especially if the society, as is the case in the US, has previously shown itself to be a pluralistic one.[19]

While Walzer is well-known for his justification of immigration restrictions, he also offers specific redress for the undocumented resident alien refugee once inside the bordered territory. He acknowledges that there are special groups that need extra protection, and access, to the bordered nation-state, especially when seen as a place of refuge. Walzer recognizes the claims of undocumented refugees for membership in the nation-state as particularly compelling, but he avers that the nation-state retains the right to determine admission.

18. Walzer, *Spheres of Justice*, 29, 40, 61–62.
19. Bosniak, *The Citizen and the Alien*, 41n12.

Part 2: Residing as an Undocumented Refugee

Nevertheless, as Bosniak discusses, Walzer supports the rights of immigrants who reside and work within the nation-state to be treated as full members of that community. And if they are not yet full members, or citizens, they should be placed on a "swift track" to citizenship.[20] Walzer writes that "every immigrant and every resident [must be] a citizen too, or at least a potential citizen" lest they fall into a sociopolitical situation of oppression under the nation-state that would be "nothing short of tyranny."[21]

Walzer's concern over the tyranny of the ruling class stems from the example he cites of ancient Athens where the "metic" caste of noncitizen resident aliens lived with no hope of ever becoming citizens of the Athenian *polis*. They bore the burden of citizenry, having to pay taxes to the *polis*, but enjoyed none of its benefits, nor protections. Like Agamben's *homo sacer* of ancient Rome, who had no status in society and could even be killed with impunity, the metic resident alien was discriminated against as a noncitizen with no recourse or claim to equal treatment with citizens. They were a second-class caste. Any children born to them became metic as well.

The status of the metic caste has some similarities with that of the undocumented resident alien in America today—but the alien in America has more hope. For example, one's US immigration status can change upon application and approval—although, for the resident undocumented alien, the application process requires leaving the US for ten years—and then be granted reentry rights with asylum status when the waiting period ends. In addition, children born in the US to refugees are deemed US citizens regardless of the citizenship of their parents.

Unlike the metics, future generations of people born in the US can find relief from the second-class caste that metics experienced. But for the long-term resident undocumented refugee, admission to the citizenship club is not guaranteed. We can condemn the metic system because our constitutional democracy does not tolerate creating a permanent subgroup of humanity. And we can join Walzer

20. Bosniak, *The Citizen and the Alien*, 41.
21. Walzer, *Spheres of Justice*, 62.

State Sovereignty and the Rights of the Resident Alien

in advocating that long-term undocumented resident alien refugees acquire citizenship status in order to bring all long-term residents onto equal footing in the eyes of the law. Considered in this light, a compassionate response to the undocumented refugee has underpinnings in an ethical analysis of equity among all long-term residents of a society who contribute to the common good.

While Walzer and Bosniak find common ground in the preference of citizen over metic, or more basely, over bare life, Esther Reed understands Agamben's bare life concept as being capable of remedy by the recognition of human rights, rather than granting citizenship[22]—a far smaller step. This more gradualist position recognizes that the unauthorized resident alien refugee, protected by alienage laws, even if undocumented, has societal value greater than bare life, and a political leg to stand on.

Though Reed was not arguing in terms of "metics," the Bosniak/Walzer metic analogy may be the more accurate description for the unauthorized resident alien than bare life, in that the resident alien in America does have certain constitutional personhood rights. The assertion of alienage rights in America can mean the difference between an illegal immigrant being granted the right to a bail hearing and potential release as opposed to languishing in prison for months without a trial.

A practical question remains. If an undocumented refugee is not given the protective status of an alien while residing in the US, how helpful are human rights to that person in face of the immigration law enforcement powers of civil government? For example, there does not seem to be a human right to peaceful existence within the territory for undocumented refugees. They risk arrest and removal from society at any time, no matter the duration of their residence. Walzer condemns the persistent threat of deportation experienced by undocumented resident aliens as a form of "membership imperialism," an overreaching of the sovereign's membership control sphere.[23] The ever-present threat of

---

22. Reed, *Theology for International Law*, 228–29n20.
23. Bosniak, *The Citizen and the Alien*, 45.

Part 2: Residing as an Undocumented Refugee

being removed from the society of the nation-state impairs the alien's ability to exercise what few civil rights he or she may have.

Exercising one's rights through the court system or in seeking social welfare benefits also means exposing one's presence, and for the undocumented resident alien refugee, such disclosure is a perilous risk to take. Yet Walzer does not go so far as to compel refugees to seek citizen status, or urge that citizenship be granted for all undocumented refugee resident aliens. Rather, he goes only so far as to provide for a citizenship "potential."[24]

Following on from this trajectory, congregants might choose to advocate for the right of the undocumented resident refugee to apply for citizenship after a certain number of years of residency in the US. Advocating for undocumented refugees spares them exposure while acting to change immigration laws in ways that would create a more just environment. Such a remedy would offer peace and stability to the refugee at minimal risk to the *polis*. It would also allow the undocumented refugee permanency and a nation-state to call home.

Refugees' Rights under Civil Law

Having identified the risks and realities of social exclusion experienced in bare life and metic classes, what rights pertain to undocumented resident refugees in the US as defined under federal law? While the broadly inclusive United Nation Convention's definition for "refugee" remains useful for our analysis, it is interesting to note that until 1980, the US limited its definition of "refugee" under the Immigration and Nationality Act[25] exclusively to address those people fleeing communist regimes. Refugees were recognized for one variety of political persecution only.[26] Under the 1980 Refugee Act,[27] the US Congress adopted a specific amendment to its defi-

---

24. Walzer, *Spheres of Justice*, 59.
25. U.S. Immigration and Nationality Act of 1952, 8 U.S.C. 1101 et seq.
26. Tichenor, *Dividing Lines*, 244.
27. U.S. Refugee Act of 1980, 8 U.S.C. ch. 12.

nition of "refugee" in order to broaden the meaning of "refugee" under US law to be more in keeping with the UN Convention and include those people fleeing political, racial, and religious persecution. The political element was not lost, but the categories of relief from other persecutions were expanded.

What was new in 1980 was a right of "asylum." For the first time there was a category of refugee called "asylees." As discussed earlier, unlike the refugee who applies for refuge from abroad, the asylee is a person who applies for asylum while already on American soil, but still must prove all refugee criteria, or be expelled.[28] Thus, asylum-seekers residing in the US may apply for asylum, but in order to be granted legal protection, they must be granted asylee status in order to stay, and apply for asylum within one year of arrival.

More than one million refugees were admitted to the US as asylees within the first decade of the inception of the 1980 Refugee Act. Under the Immigration Act of 1990, the annual immigration level was further increased. However, tolerance from US citizens concerning the influx of refugees did not keep pace. It was a time of rapid immigration expansion in the US, despite the preferences of ordinary citizens to clamp down on access to the US. A rise in nationalism and resentments among certain citizens stoked tensions among communities where legal immigrants were arriving in greater numbers.[29] By 1994, anti-immigration voices began winning legislative measures at the ballot box as a new wave of American nativist sentiment appeared in communities where immigrants were moving in.

In pursuing a just Christian immigration ethic, nationalism has no place in the equation. Instead, as we have come to understand in our definition of "refugee," those who flee persecution are precious life created by God. The refugee has human rights and human characteristics that we share. Our goal as Christians is to discern an ethic of hospitality that welcomes the refugee already in our midst. Under the lordship of Christ in the political realm, witnesses to God's purposes for humanity, we are called to advocate

28. Daniels, *Guarding the Golden Door*, 204.
29. Tichenor, *Dividing Lines*, 245.

Part 2: Residing as an Undocumented Refugee

for government laws and policies that promote peace, freedom, and justice. What does this look like in terms of the undocumented resident refugee?

Thinking theologically about our nation-state's immigration and alienage policies entails a reframing of our approach. For example, how we think about the alien in theological terms is significantly different from the way we understand the resident alien under US alienage laws. To this point, Robert Heimburger observes that describing a people as "alien" is simply not "truthful" in the eyes of God. Theologically speaking, God, as loving creator and sovereign, is working through Christ to bring all people together from far and near through the power of the Spirit.[30] There are no aliens in the eyes of God. Similarly, there are no illegal people. There are merely illegal actions, classifications, and relationships with respect to the nation-state.

Heimburger maintains that the centrality of law and order in America has led to the over-politicization of American life, forcing people into legal categories of alien or citizen, legal or illegal. As a political theologian, Heimburger encourages us, instead, to take a view of refugees as being in solidarity with the church: "reminding her that she is a community of sojourners . . . a people en-lawed in Christ, becoming like the members of the many peoples of the world so that they might share in the fruits of the gospel."[31] Or, as Stanley Hauerwas argues, we are all foreigners in a foreign land—doing our best to maintain our Christian faith in our everyday lives while living in a fallen world.[32] Heimburger identifies the tension between law and order in civic affairs and obedience to God's sovereignty in the kingdom of Christ. He encourages congregants to side with Christ in ministering to the refugee.

The tension between church and state intensifies when the laws of the nation-state become corrupted, no longer pursuing justice, but rather are used as the tools of totalitarian leadership. Although Reformer John Calvin had barely begun to develop a

---

30. Heimburger, *God and the Illegal Alien*, 61.
31. Heimburger, *God and the Illegal Alien*, 61.
32. Hauerwas, *Vision and Virtue*, 47.

response to the unjust nation-state in his *Institutes* for situations where civil magistrates pervert justice and the nation-state becomes corrupt, [33] Karl Barth wrote extensively on it as a result of living through the conflictual era beginning with the First World War and continuing through the Cold War.

Barth addresses the tension between church and state differently from Heimburger and Hauerwas. Barth focused on reconciling church and state as symbiotic parts of God's realm, rather than holding the church's ministry to the refugee as a remedy apart, as Heimburger suggests, while civil society fends off threats of harm to its membership.[34] Nor does Barth see the church as a separate alien existence implanted in a fallen society, as Hauerwas would claim under the emergent tradition, where the church does not exist as an "ethos for democracy," but rather provides an alternative to every nation, witnessing to the existence that is "possible for those who have been formed by the story of Christ."[35] Instead, Barth relies on Christ's sovereign rule as the center of all things, including for both the church and every nation-state.

In his essay "The Christian Community and the Civil Community," a work which reverberates with his struggle with the German Church under the Nazi regime from 1933 to 1945, Barth famously describes the relationship of church, state, and Christ as a series of concentric circles—with Christ at the center, the church encircling Christ, and the outside world orbiting around the church.[36] They are all connected, interdependent, yet distinct.

The church has the role of witness and prophetic voice for the state, to keep it "just" in accordance with Christ's purposes for human flourishing. At the same time, the church is still in need of its own redeeming. The nation-state, on the other hand, is a purely civil community, ignorant of God's kingdom and indifferent to the faith of the church in Christ. Thus, the nation-state needs the Christian community in order to execute its political

---

33. Kraus, "The Contemporary Relevance," 325.
34. Heimburger, *God and the Illegal Alien*, 211.
35. Hauerwas, *A Community of Character*, 1.
36. Barth, *Community*, 169.

Part 2: Residing as an Undocumented Refugee

responsibility—arguably, it needs the church in order to know what its political responsibility is.[37] The role of the church, then, is to model what true justice looks like.

Barth's experience navigating in and around Nazi Germany led to his leadership in drafting the Theological Declaration of Barmen[38] in 1934 with a Confessional Synod of German churches to protest the fascist Nazi regime that took over both the German nation-state and the churches within it. This creedal confession was eventually adopted by Presbyterian and Reformed churches worldwide. Its primary goal was to encourage the "Evangelical churches" of Germany to stand firm against the popular movement of "German Christians" who "saw no conflict between Christianity and the ideals of Hitler's National Socialism."[39] The German Confessing Church, those opposing the German Christians of the "German Church," adopted the Declaration of Barmen and supported its proclamation of "the church's freedom in Jesus Christ who is Lord of every area of life."[40] The Declaration of Barmen includes the commitment never to permit any head of state to replace Christ as head of the church, or as revelation of God's truth, or as a minister of Christ's church.[41]

With the German Church corrupted by Nazi propaganda, there was no one to stand up against the demonic force of the encroaching unjust state—except for other churches outside Germany, and the courageous protesters of the German Confessing Church. Perhaps for this reason Barth held on tightly to the notion that the church must always be prepared to serve as witness, reminder, and even scourge to the civil community where it is located, to proclaim God's higher purposes of justice and dignity for all.

37. Barth, *Community*, 169–70.

38. "The Theological Declaration of Barmen" was written by 139 delegates, including Karl Barth, collectively representing the Lutheran, Reformed, and United churches in *Gemarke* Church, Barmen, in the City of Wupperthal, May 29–31, 1934. The full text is available in Presbyterian Church (USA)'s *Book of Confessions*, 280–84.

39. *Book of Confessions*, 280.

40. *Book of Confessions*, 280.

41. Declaration of Barmen, §§ 8.12, 8.15, 8.21.

The corruption of the German Church had another invisible consequence: the loss of an advocate for the refugee. In Germany, the refugee was not the person trying to enter, but the German-born who had their citizenship stripped away because of their religion, political opposition, or sexual orientation. In other neighboring nations as well, the conflict of the Second World War created many more refugees facing statelessness and the loss of a place in the *polis*. They had no nation-state to call home, no passport to travel on, and no membership right to claim in any society anywhere. When the German Church fell to Nazi influence as well, there was no one left to advocate for those stripped of their citizenship and made stateless: the Jews, the dissidents, the homosexuals, and the community of nomadic "Romas." They were stateless bare life; and without an advocate from church or any nation-state, they were exterminated.

The Refugee as Stateless

During World War II, and even in the aftermath of World War I, many European nations denaturalized and denationalized large numbers of their own populations. The resulting "statelessness" of the refugees fleeing these war-torn nation-states was experienced first-hand by Jewish political philosopher Hannah Arendt. She fled for her life from Nazi Germany without a passport, or the right to one, despite being born in Germany. She had been stripped of her citizenship under the totalitarian Nazi regime. She lived as a refugee in France, stateless, until being interned in a refugee camp there during the German occupation. Arendt managed to escape the prison camp and flee to America where she continued to live a stateless existence until granted US citizenship in 1951. Her life experience greatly informed her work on the problems of refugees, and the dimension of statelessness that reduces the refugee to a "bare life" existence.

Arendt described the death spiral from citizen to statelessness experienced by war refugees in chilling terms.

Part 2: Residing as an Undocumented Refugee

> [The problem of statelessness for refugees] . . . is not that they are not equal before the law, but that no law exists for them . . . Only in the last stage of a rather lengthy process is their right to live threatened; only if they remain "superfluous," if nobody can be found to "claim" them may their lives be in danger. Even the Nazis started their extermination of the Jews by first depriving them of all legal status (the status of second-class citizenship) and cutting them off from the world of the living by herding them into ghettos and concentration camps; and before they set the gas chambers into motion they had carefully tested the ground and found out to their satisfaction that no country would claim these people. The point is that a condition of complete rightlessness was created before the right to life was challenged.[42]

Reducing a person to stateless, bare life carries no rights, no territorial personhood, and, thus, no right to live. Arendt's observations and firsthand experiences as a stateless person make it even more apparent how important alienage laws can be, even if inadequate—even if made subordinate to the membership controls of the nation-state.[43]

If refugees enter within the bordered territory, they merit some basic level of protections: at a very minimum, the right to life itself. How we evaluate our welcome of undocumented refugees in America always needs to be tempered by this minimalist extreme. If we ignore the children held in detention centers at our southern borders when families are separated, or when refugee children arrive alone, we risk losing them to a system that lacks accountability. But inside our gates, their rights as refugees shift from immigrant to alien. It is there that legal hope lies in America.

---

42. Arendt, *The Origins of Totalitarianism*, 295–96.

43. Arendt's measure of the desperation of refugees and the test of whether they have fallen outside the pale of the law altogether was whether it was beneficial for the stateless person to commit a crime. "Since the [stateless person] was an anomaly for which the law did not provide, it was better for him to become an anomaly for which the state did provide, that of the criminal." Arendt, *The Origins of Totalitarianism*, 286.

State Sovereignty and the Rights of the Resident Alien

There is a legal framework in the US to protect stateless, rightless, undocumented refugee resident aliens from being forgotten and discarded, so long as caring individuals, journalists, lawyers and lawmakers, clergy members, congregants, and all citizens advocate for them. Together we can make their presence known and claim them as our own with compassionate hearts, recognizing them first as God's beloved human beings, then as aliens with legal rights, and finally as our neighbors in need.

Sovereignty of the Nation-State

The realities of a refugee's existence being stripped to bare life and the statelessness concerns of nonexistence expressed by Hannah Arendt are stop-gapped in the US legal environment by the existence of alienage laws. The basic human rights of an alien, even if undocumented, as set out in our Constitution and in case law, can protect those refugees who do make it inside US territory even if unauthorized for residence.

Between immigration and alienage laws, there is a middle ground where the nation-state can balance entrance deterrence and asylum rights of unauthorized refugees who settle in the US. But there are ways to receive and assess asylum-seeker applications in ways that are more humane and welcoming than what has been experienced at the US border with Mexico in recent years. When US immigration policies obliterate the human rights of the refugee, or the alien rights of the long-term undocumented residents, US citizen congregants can agitate for policy changes by exercising their right to vote on immigration issues, advocating for the refugee, and speaking out for justice. Engaging in the democratic process is one step US citizen congregants can take towards developing a just Christian ethic of immigration in America.

But there is more to consider. Congregants can be informed by insights from political theology in making ethical decisions about the treatment of the undocumented resident alien refugee as well. One task of political theology is to measure how well our civil governance responds to God's sovereign claim over all

Part 2: Residing as an Undocumented Refugee

creation—and God's salvific hope for God's people through Jesus Christ. We turn now to this assessment in the following study of God's sovereign claim over all creation.

Chapter 4

The Sovereignty of God and the Polity of the Common Good

[Jesus asked the lawyer] "Which of these three, do you think, was a neighbor to the man who fell into the hands of the robbers?" He said, "The one who showed him mercy." Jesus said to him, "Go and do likewise."

—Luke 10:35–36 (NRSV)

"CITY OF GOD": POLITICAL THEOLOGY, GOD'S SOVEREIGNTY, AND THE COMMON GOOD

WHAT DOES POLITICAL THEOLOGY tell us about refugee welcome as discerning Christians? What impact should the sovereignty of God play on the way we govern our nation-state and treat the long-term resident undocumented refugee? Through the larger lens of

Part 2: Residing as an Undocumented Refugee

God at work in our common life together, we can begin to reflect not so much on whether, but rather on why and how we might offer refugees welcome within our bordered nation.

Having established above that there are inconsistencies in the civil laws around the rights of aliens and the nation-state's control over immigration, I suggested that political advocacy for legislative change could provide undocumented refugees a pathway to citizenship. Understanding that change is possible, we can begin to think ethically about why improving the legal environment for refugee welcome is important. In this chapter we consider sovereignty, and the undocumented refugee resident alien, in theological terms, thinking as political theologians. In order to promote ethical nation-state actions towards the resident alien undocumented refugee, we assess the nation-state as a *polis* and God's people, divided into nations, as all being under God's sovereign care.

Augustine: God's Sovereignty for the Common Good

Although Augustine, a Roman African and early Christian theologian (354–430 CE), lived just over a thousand years before the Reformation, his theological understanding of God's creation and relationship with humanity provided important undergirding for the conceptual theological framework of later Reformed theologians. One such cornerstone is the central place of law in society as needful for God's greater purposes. We will now consider God's greater purposes in our discernment of a just Christian immigration ethic.

In *City of God*, Augustine describes the sovereignty of God over all creation, differentiating the City of God from the earthly cities. The members of the City of God worship God, and turn their focus away from themselves. Augustine contrasts the City of God with the earthly cities whose members focus on themselves, and turn away from God.[1] Augustine explains that the resolution of this division comes through Christ's redemption. People are

---

1. Augustine, *City of God*, XV/7:604.

The Sovereignty of God and the Polity of the Common Good

sinful, but through Christ they can still find fulfillment in universal communion with God. It is the communion with, and connection to, God that is at the heart of God's greater purposes for our common life together—the community that includes everyone.

Luke Bretherton explains this Augustinian framework further:

> For Augustine, it is the ends or loves of the polity which form the basis of its common life. Thus, the difference between the earthly city and the City of God rests in their different ends or objects of love. An earthly city cannot be a true *res publica* because the nature of its loves means that it can never be a truly harmonious society; rather, it always involves individual and group competition and hostility. For Augustine, the politics of any instance of the earthly city is about negotiating what is necessary for a tolerable earthly peace to exist within which the Gospel can be preached and which the heavenly city makes use of for a time. The earthly city is not an end in itself, but serves an end—communion with God—beyond itself.[2]

Bretherton goes on to apply this earthly city model to the *polis* of the modern nation-state, affirming that "[t]he role of political authority is to establish the conditions for human flourishing through the promulgation and enforcement of law."[3] In this way, the confluence of law and society provides a place in which God can be worshipped and humanity can thrive as God's creatures, in communion with God and each other. The civil nation-state and the purposes of God can work together when both church and *polis* share the common goal of building up the common good of society.

In formulating this idea of community life, Augustine begins with the household as the model, or starting place, for the *polis*. He argues that the established peace of one's home spreads outward to the greater community.[4] But at the same time, our humanity gets in our own way: violence, jealousies, and selfish behaviors proliferate. As ethicist Jean Elshtain describes it, the need for earthly rule

---

2. Bretherton, "The Duty of Care," 49.
3. As cited in Bretherton, "The Duty of Care," 49.
4. Augustine, *City of God*, XIX/16:876.

Part 2: Residing as an Undocumented Refugee

derives from human sinfulness, and thus, we must erect barriers and provide protection from each other.[5] After the fall, Augustine's idea goes, earthly cities formed to make more manageable earthly life. But into this secular realm, God provides humanity with *caritas*, the loving grace of God, that gives hope, and a gateway, through Christ, to reconnect with our creator, a path available to Christian and non-Christian alike.[6]

Against the background of life in the *polis*, we are also reminded from our earlier discussion on border walls that the primary need of the refugee is political: belonging in a peaceful, stable community, governed by the rule of law. Bretherton notes that, as a matter of political theology, following on Augustine's teaching, the purpose of having an orderly polity is to provide a place of peace in which God can be rightly worshipped and where community members can be in communion with God. Yet, he acknowledges the challenge for liberal democracies, such as the US, is to maintain, or even establish, a God-centered *telos*. Instead, our communities tend to prefer worshipping themselves.

This tendency for a self-centered, rather than Christ-centered, outlook on life makes it all the harder for churches and congregations to witness effectively to legislators the need for laws that welcome undocumented refugees who have been residing in the US for long periods of time.

> Liberal democracies are good insofar as they provide a limited peace. However, as the treatment of asylum-seekers makes clear, they have made an end in and of themselves and their common lives are based on objects of love—notably, individual and collective self-fulfillment and autonomy—that inherently tend towards hostility to needy strangers. They tend towards hostility to needy strangers because the pursuit of such goods directs us away from the just and generous consideration of the needs of others. Yet, on a conception of the polity within the Christian tradition, there should be no

---

5. Elshtain, *Sovereignty*, 9.
6. Elshtain, *Sovereignty*, 9.

incompatibility between welcoming refugees and pursuit of the common life of the polity.[7]

As Christians, we must constantly strive to look towards fulfilling the needs of others in ways that enhance the common good.

Reformed theology equates a lawful polity with a just society that permits God's people to flourish in right relationship with God. Reformer John Calvin used the tools of law and order to promote a Christian city in Geneva that welcomed refugees. Reformed churches today have similar proclivities: preserving law and order while finding a way to welcome the refugee, even the undocumented one. It may help congregants who are uncomfortable with the unlawful aspect of an undocumented refugee's status to remember that illegal status does not make the refugee an illegal person. The refugee is God's creation—as such, we, citizens and undocumented aliens, alike, are united through Christ. Our actions and attitudes should reflect this theological stance of unity.

Applying political theology to nation-state sovereignty over immigration law removes the scales from our eyes. We can see what we are up against in finding a "tolerable earthly peace." If we are to have law and order and a nation-state, not every migrant can be admitted. But for those refugees who have already entered, whether legally or not, the question of welcome and assimilation into the polity is a separate one. The undocumented long-term resident refugee has been absorbed into society and is a peaceful member of it. But every undocumented resident refugee needs membership rights, political belonging, and the benefits that go with them in order to be free from the fear of removal and to flourish in the common life of the community. It is this common life within the Christian tradition to which we now turn as members of the *polis*, discerning a way to welcome the long-term resident undocumented refugee while preserving the good of all.

---

7. Bretherton, "The Duty of Care," 49.

Part 2: Residing as an Undocumented Refugee

Common Ground in the Common Good

Secular sovereignty should mean something more than a nation-state's power over its borders and control over its entrance policies. It should also include an indefatigable pursuit of what is best for the common life of all its members, recognizing the humanity of every one of them, not just a few, and not at the expense of a subclass of people who fail to qualify for citizenship. Churches and congregants can find hope in the common Christian teleology that "orders the good of a particular community as being fulfilled in the good of humanity which is itself fulfilled in communion with God."[8]

Thus, promoting the common good, through a polity that recognizes the rule of law, can connect us in relationship with our neighbor, and with God. But we must work together through our church communities in order to make progress along a Christian path that advocates for refugee welcome against the grain of an inward-looking secular world.

To pursue this path of progress, churches and congregants can be considering ways to promote the common good of the nation-state from a Christian ethics perspective. Looking realistically at numbers of refugees and the abundance of local resources, congregants should be asking whether the human flourishing of all can still be achieved within a peaceful *polis* when the undocumented refugee is introduced into the community. To resolve this question, churches and congregants may want to revisit borders, this time in terms of transcending them, to help their neighbors far and near.

ORDERED LOVES AND THE REFORMED TRADITION'S TREATMENT OF THE REFUGEE

Christian ethicist Esther Reed asks the practical question of which neighbors one should help: near or far, citizen or refugee? Reed addresses the challenge of the new form of cosmopolitanism that weighs the interests of the citizen and refugee equally, as a balance

---

8. Bretherton, *Christianity and Contemporary Politics*, 131.

The Sovereignty of God and the Polity of the Common Good

of equities favoring the common good, while still respecting the nation-state's need for a bordered territory.[9] What's at stake for Reed is whether the traditional *ordo amoris*, or ordered loves, that Augustine posits, favoring the proximate neighbor, as described in more detail below, continues to have a place in Christian ethics, or whether it should be replaced by a universal benevolence to everyone.[10] The question of ordered loves also touches on the Reformed tradition's understanding of the doctrine of creation—the way we relate to one another as God's creatures and as neighbors to one another. This concept merits our further consideration of refugees as neighbors, whether living far away in other states or near to us in our neighborhoods.

Augustine and "Ordered Loves" in the Modern Day

To understand how the idea of "ordered loves" applies to the question of welcoming the resident undocumented refugee, it helps to have some theological background. The idea of *ordo amoris* comes from the Christian tradition that one cannot, in practice, love all people equally. Augustine expressed it in his treatise *On Christian Doctrine* this way:

> [A]ll people should be loved equally. But you cannot do good to all people equally, so you should take particular thought for those who by the chance of place or time, or anything else, are, as if by lot, in particularly close contact with you.[11]

Thus, since we cannot love all equally, we must discern which people to give priority. Augustine suggests that loving our most proximate neighbor is the fair and practical way to proceed.

Augustine's cosmopolitan vision of universal love for neighbor, and privileging those in our proximity, is a highly practical approach to the overwhelming and impossible needs of our many

---

9. Reed, *Theology for International Law*, 222.
10. Reed, *Theology for International Law*, 229.
11. Augustine, *De Doctrina Christiana*, 61.

Part 2: Residing as an Undocumented Refugee

neighbors in the world. And, as Reed points out, the harshness of choosing near over far neighbor is softened by the knowledge that there are ostensibly others living at a distance who are neighbors to those far away and in need.[12] Thus, if all agree to help the nearest neighbor the world over, no one should be left out.

Reed preserves the notion of prioritizing neighbor love based on proximity, after a thorough analysis that rejects favoritism based on kinship, nationalism, or immoral partiality, in order to be realistic about the need for moral action and response to the neighbor who lives next door, who just might be an undocumented refugee.[13] Ultimately, Reed reminds us, God judges the relative morality of every human action or inaction. It is Christ who mediates every interaction between self and other. We must make our own choices, but Reed would seem to advise a preference for the near neighbor—the refugee in the neighborhood ahead of the refugee at the border wall.

The *polis* itself can be a resource in acting on neighbor love. And so can the church. Congregants would find increased effectiveness in joining together, as a church, to engage in group political action in their community after identifying their refugee neighbors, their needs, and how best to love them. Joint action, neighborly welcome, and the Spirit at work among a collaborative church and healthy community can provide a kick-start to meaningful refugee welcome.

Karl Barth—Neighbors Far and Near

Reformed theologian Karl Barth returns the conversation to the conceptual in his treatment of God's command to love our neighbors far and near. But in this instance, near neighbors refer not merely to proximate individuals, but also to people groupings divided into nations.[14] Wrestling with the meaning of nations within

---

12. Reed, *Theology for International Law*, 221.
13. Reed, *Theology for International Law*, 246.
14. Barth, *CD* III/4:309–23.

The Sovereignty of God and the Polity of the Common Good

God's command to love neighbor far and near, Barth warns against embracing either an abstract cosmopolitanism or an abstract nationalism, but rather to recognize that "all nations are of one blood"—destined to be reunited in Christ.[15]

Barth pursues the biblical story of humanity through to the New Testament and the greater salvation history of God. With the revelation of God in Christ and the miracle experienced through the Holy Spirit among the apostles at Pentecost, the unity of neighbors far and near becomes more apparent. The Spirit draws people together while at once causing them to reach out to others from afar.

As Robert Heimburger observed in commenting on Barth's biblical discussion of neighbors far and near, the Holy Spirit enables the apostles to move outwards to their far neighbors. "It is a work of the Spirit, not a human being, to build this bridge from those nearby to those far away.[16]" Heimburger goes beyond Barth to emphasize the preservation of cultural and racial diversity. He remarks that the Spirit at Pentecost appeared to allow a new Israel to form, "speaking the one Word about the Risen Christ in many languages."[17]

In any setting, the rich creaturely life is one that is oriented towards others, so that, through Christ, we can connect with one another and with God. It is this communion together with God through Christ that Barth posits as the driver of relationships among peoples. Quoting Ephesians 2:13, Barth rests his case: those who have felt far off have been brought near in Jesus Christ. Heimburger adds: "migrants can be called distant neighbors coming near" as well.[18]

The command of God is for humans to be in fellowship, both near and far. Our neighborly obligations have no bounds, nor does our shared personhood have boundaries. As a result, we are called as Christians to welcome the refugee neighbor who comes

15. Barth, *CD* III/4:312–13.
16. Heimburger, *God and the Illegal Alien*, 50.
17. Heimburger, *God and the Illegal Alien*, 50.
18. Heimburger, *God and the Illegal Alien*, 53.

Part 2: Residing as an Undocumented Refugee

to reside among us from afar—even if arriving without authorization. There is an expectation of our offering welcome and the Spirit leads us in that welcoming. But the actions each one of us takes with respect to the stranger is for us each to determine in freedom and in covenant with God.

Barth describes God as showing such overflowing love and grace that God created humanity as a distinct existence with which to share God's joy. These joyful experiences are to love and be loved, to be in relationship with God and with neighbor, to receive the grace of Jesus Christ through the power of the Holy Spirit, and to seek out the flourishing of God's creation, including each individual person. Barth's doctrinal understanding of the divine and human interrelationship provides the theological basis for offering welcome to the stranger, even if an undocumented refugee.

Working towards the common good as an expression of our faith leads us to question what is morally right or wrong at our borders, how we should treat our neighbors, be they far or near, and what kind of welcome a refugee should receive in our hometowns regardless of visa status. Competing claims among citizen, alien, and refugee for life, freedom, and compassion makes the question of Christian ethics at the borders, in our towns, and in our homes an interconnected one. The Reformed tradition's response to this common plea for a peaceable existence demands not only careful reflection, but also a commitment to action: to do the most good for the most people in our common life together in communion with God.

If we can accept this Christian commitment to take action to welcome the undocumented refugee into the community for the common good, then one question remains in the process of discernment for congregants and churches. What does a practical theology of welcome look like? In other words, how do churches, church leaders, and their congregants ethically welcome their near neighbor who is an undocumented refugee? We will find practical answers and options to consider in the pages that follow.

SUMMARY OF PART 2

Part 2 of our study offered perspectives for separating human lives from legal classifications, and civil laws from sacred duties. In examining US laws on immigration and alienage, chapter 4 revealed that there are basic constitutional protections for aliens, such as due process rights and bail bond rights for refugees in detention, that elevate the undocumented refugee up from a bare life existence once residing in the US, even if maintaining a residence without authorization. Reinforcing this legitimate basis for offering refugee welcome under the alienage laws of the nation-state, chapter 5 established that the sovereign laws of God promote fellowship among neighbors, far and near, in working towards the common good.

Finding that both the goals of the nation-state and the purposes of God can work together through community-building for human flourishing, churches and congregants now have law and faith-based reasons to welcome their neighbor refugees, regardless of their legal status. Reformed faith communities, especially, have support from a long history of Reformed theologians who understand the refugee as a distant neighbor come near whom Christians are called to welcome with merciful care under God's covenant doctrine of faithfulness. Moreover, the nation-states themselves have an obligation of mercifulness in welcoming refugees. The nation-state is intended, by God, to be just. There are times when the church must remind the nation-state of its loftier goals towards peace, justice, and the flourishing of everyone in community.

Our overview of US alienage and immigration laws and introduction to political theology in the Reformed tradition provides churches and congregants an ethical basis from which to formulate an active, ethical plan of refugee welcome in their own communities. Now equipped with a just immigration ethic to support refugee welcome, churches need only determine how best to welcome the long-term resident undocumented refugee in their neighborhoods. The following chapters offer practical guidance

Part 2: Residing as an Undocumented Refugee

for welcoming our refugee neighbors, even those who lack authorization to reside in the US communities that they call home.

Part 3

Abiding with the Undocumented Refugee

Chapter 5

A Christian Ethic of Worship, Witness, and Welcome

"But now, in Christ Jesus, you who once were far off have been brought near by the blood of Christ."

—Eph 2:13 (NRSV)

INTRODUCTION

HAVING ESTABLISHED THAT THE goals of the nation-state and the purposes of God align in the objective of supporting the common good for the flourishing of all humanity, including the undocumented refugee, these final chapters explore ways for churches and congregants to make refugee welcome a reality in their communities. By acknowledging that undocumented resident refugees are proximate neighbors in need, bereft of membership in the society, congregants and churches can find ways to welcome the refugees residing in their neighborhoods. This chapter attends to

Part 3: Abiding with the Undocumented Refugee

the question: "What can our church do to welcome our undocumented neighbor refugee?"

The Reformed faith tradition privileges legal means of welcoming the refugee, but acknowledges, as Barth did, that there are times and places when the church must witness to God's preeminent call for justice, essentially modeling for the nation-state what true justice should look like. The legal status of the refugee does not determine the decision about how to welcome once the refugee is understood as a person who is not *malum in se*, but rather is one who engaged in prohibited conduct and lacks a legal category to remain in the US.

Accepting the personhood of the undocumented refugee as God's beloved creation permits churches and congregants to focus on ways of restoring that person to full membership in the community of God. In this chapter I suggest three methods of doing so: (i) finding common ground in worship, (ii) witnessing to just immigration policies, and (iii) offering a welcome that both forgives and connects the outcast resident refugee to the inclusive community of Christ. Not all undocumented refugees need be Christian to be welcomed, but all Christians should be welcoming of the refugee neighbor in this expansive way. In order to find the strength and courage to do so, congregants can begin at church. Through worship and church fellowship, the power of the Holy Spirit can slowly transform a congregation from hesitation to action in welcoming the resident undocumented refugee.

CHRISTIAN WORSHIP: WELCOMING THE REFUGEE HOME

The church, when gathered at worship, creates a communal body—a political body in its own right—that serves as Christ's counterpoint to the social and economic pressures that secular practices impose on our lives. It is in Christ-centered worship, with attention to Scripture, sermon, sacrament, and prayer where Christians are reminded of their duty of care to the other, driven by God's love of all creation. As Bretherton notes:

A Christian Ethic of Worship, Witness, and Welcome

> If it is the dynamics of the nation-state that render refugees as bare life, it is the dynamics of worship ... that serve as a preliminary preparation for encountering the refugee as neighbor.[1]

Significantly, what worship, and the practices of listening to Scripture and sermon, and sharing in the sacraments, can produce in the congregant is the starting place for a moral conversion, a transformation, that enables him or her to recognize the long-term resident undocumented refugee as "neighbor." Fed by the Spirit through worship, congregants can then pursue compassionate action on behalf of the refugee in the throes of a contested political issue over who's in and who's out.

The Reformed tradition emphasizes the authority of Scripture as a starting place to find guidance for our actions as followers of Christ. Listening to Scripture helps church congregants discern God's living Word for their lives today. In his *Institutes*, Calvin emphasizes two "marks" by which the church can be recognized (signs that bring the otherwise "invisible" church into reality and relevance)—and they both occur in worship:

> [W]here we see the Word of God purely preached and heard, and the sacraments administered according to Christ's institution, there ... the church of God exists.[2]

Given this emphasis on authentic communion with God through Scripture and sermon, churches in the Reformed tradition, especially, will want to begin their preparation for neighbor love and refugee welcome through the word read and proclaimed. Because Scripture is open to the work of the Holy Spirit in the interpretation, application, and communication of God's will for our lives, hearing Scripture in worship allows congregants to open themselves up to the possibility of transformation. The Spirit at work can bring a congregant from a place of feeling hostility towards the stranger to a realignment towards acceptance of the undocumented neighbor refugee.

---

1. Bretherton, *Christianity and Contemporary Politics*, 143.
2. Calvin, *Institutes* IV.i.9:1023.

Part 3: Abiding with the Undocumented Refugee

Worship, as a means of preparing the congregation to recognize and embrace the neighbor refugee, begins with words from Scripture, first read, and then proclaimed. The sermon proclamation is the centerpiece of worship in the Reformed liturgical tradition, and it is this homiletic treatment of Scripture that can be most transformative in the life of the listening congregation. Through sermonic teaching, explaining, and exhorting, the preacher can develop meaning from Scripture texts, like the parable of the Good Samaritan, and offer its application to the everyday lives of modern hearers. The sermon is where preachers can teach and encourage neighbor love and identify the resident refugee as a neighbor deserving welcome, even if that neighbor lacks documentation for legal status to stay.

The preacher's task is to address the tension between the "law of God" and "law of *polis*" and to encourage congregants to act with more mercy than does the nation-state. Sermons can inspire congregants to consider long-term resident undocumented refugees in a new light of forgiveness—and accept that their refugee neighbors have already forged a life within the border walls. These neighbors are no longer outsiders but have come to live within the *polis* without destabilizing its peace.

Nevertheless, the lives of these undocumented refugees remain in danger so long as they are reduced to bare life or excluded on a permanent basis from membership in their new community. Offering a message of mercy for the long-term resident undocumented refugee through Scripture read and word proclaimed are two elements of worship that can transform congregants to become better neighbors to the refugees nearby who are trapped in a legal limbo but would like to become citizens if they could. As Calvin insisted, the task of the preacher is to serve as the planter of the seeds of gracious faith—while God gives the congregation the gift of growth from hearing them.[3]

Beyond mere hearing, congregants ingest the very Word of God through the sacrament of holy communion and through prayer. Worshippers internalize what they have heard from

---

3. Calvin, *Institutes* IV.i.6:1021.

A Christian Ethic of Worship, Witness, and Welcome

Scripture in responding with prayer and consume God's grace by eating the bread of heaven and drinking from the cup of the new covenant at communion. These actions also invite the Spirit to enter the lives of congregants.

The sacrament of communion is a mark of grace recognized in the Reformed tradition as an active process by which God is called among us and is present in us and through us. The Holy Spirit is invited to suffuse the elements of bread and wine with grace, acting as an agent of transformation for the congregation. In receiving God's gracious mercy, forgiveness, and opportunity to live life afresh as God's redeemed creatures by the administration of the sacrament of the Lord's Supper, congregants are nourished and equipped to spread God's grace outwards to the world. With guidance from the pastor on where to look and how to engage, reaching out to the nearby neighbor refugee can become a congregation's next step of outreach to express God's gracious love.

For Christian refugees, worship life and shared communion redeems their "bare life" existence in a physical way as they rejoin others in community and are regarded as equals before God. They are reconstituted at the communion table as life relocated within, and one with, the body of Christ as full members of the congregation. Remembering Christ through communion aids the outcast refugee in re-"membering" as part of society, with a place among peers, no longer mere bare life, but a life that belongs.

Denominational policy reforms in recent years have led to an acceptance of "open table" communion in the Presbyterian Church (USA) and other Reformed churches. The *Directory of Worship of the Presbyterian Church (USA)* now specifically mandates that the Eucharist be shared with all seekers, even those people who are not yet baptized.

> The opportunity to eat and drink with Christ is not a right bestowed upon the worthy, but a privilege given to the undeserving who come in faith, repentance, and love. All who come to the table are offered the bread and cup, regardless of their age or understanding. If some of those who come have not yet been baptized, an

invitation to baptismal preparation and Baptism should be graciously extended.[4]

With willing hearts and a theology consistent with hospitable welcome, Presbyterian-Reformed church congregants can make space for the Holy Spirit and the undocumented refugee neighbor to find common ground. Small steps towards ever-deepening encounters with refugee neighbors, inviting them to worship, joining them in fellowship, and expressing neighborliness in the community, combine to initiate the personal transformation of individual congregants who find compassion and connection with refugees in their own neighborhoods.

As Christine Pohl points out in her work on Christian hospitality, we need more than worship time together to prepare our hearts to reach out to refugees as neighbors—we need connection.[5] She observes that, without significant connections, even the neediest people in our neighborhoods become invisible to us. When churches and congregants engage in the intentional process of welcoming through inclusive worship and fellowship, they raise up the dignity of the refugee to that of family. They reconfigure social relations and follow Christ's reordering of family connections. Thus, as churches move from worship to witness, congregants can begin to see their undocumented neighbor refugee as a human life worth saving.

From Worship to Fellowship with the Near Neighbor Refugee

Worship is a first step to welcome. Fellowship can and should follow when we get to know the neighbors in our pews and invite the stranger in our neighborhood to join us in Christian shared community activity. There are different approaches to finding fellowship with the stranger. As examples, the Reformed tradition tries to include the stranger in the community, first through worship

---

4. PC(USA), *Book of Order*, W3.0409.
5. Pohl, *Making Room*, 90.

A Christian Ethic of Worship, Witness, and Welcome

and communion, then through shared mission activity. But even simple acts of fellowship, neighborliness, and hospitality can change the dynamic in a community from wariness to welcome.

A Christian Ethic of Radical Hospitality

In whatever way churches and congregants approach the question of refugee welcome, offering hospitality can serve as both a political act and a Christian practice. Welcoming the outcast, undocumented refugee is an act of Christian hospitality. "Welcoming" as a Christian practice models the faith in a tangible way. It takes a stand and shows the nation-state how the relationship with refugees should be lived, even for those who are here without legal authorization. Christian hospitality is an act of faith and a political act both at once. It models a behavior that dares to welcome refugees to the community in face of laws that would remove them from the community once and for all.

In congregations that are divided over whether to welcome the undocumented refugee, the practice of Christian hospitality is an intentional means of approaching the "other," especially those with whom we disagree. Arguing that the Christian ethic of hospitality is a radical political practice, Bretherton asserts that an ethic of hospitality maintains peaceful relations in our common life together and is, thus, central to "what constitutes the good society."[6] Thus, offering hospitality, even to one who has violated the laws of the nation-state, is a gracious act that maintains the peace of the *polis*.

Ilsup Ahn, writing from the Roman Catholic tradition, describes hospitality towards the migrant as adequately "radical" only when it is tied to the forgiveness of the one being welcomed.[7] He urges that politicians adopt measures of forgiveness to include the undocumented refugees into the society of refuge. A radical hospitality of forgiveness both embraces and includes the other—and reduces cultural, political, and economic privileges that separate

---

6. Bretherton, *Hospitality as Holiness*, 126.
7. Ahn, *Religious Ethics and Migration*, 25.

Part 3: Abiding with the Undocumented Refugee

the migrant from the host. Basing his approach in Catholic Social Teaching, Ahn sees the forgiveness paradigm as the host paying off the invisible debt that the refugee bears in transgressing laws in order to remain resident in the US. He argues for implementing radical hospitality as a political approach to addressing the immigration challenges faced in the US. He considers that the political and the theological must work together to achieve positive results for the common good.

Reformed theologians more often focus on repairing the social injustices that caused the unauthorized residence of the undocumented refugee in the first place. The Reformed tradition insists on proclamation and witness to Christ's teachings in face of the wrongs done that initially created the refugee situation. Reformed churches would seek ways to change civil society to conform more closely to God's purposes, including taking political action to change unjust laws and policies that render refugees as bare life.

Equally important in Reformed theology is the redemption of the refugee from bare life by restoring human dignity and a place of belonging in society. Presbyterian-Reformed churches can be seeking ways to reestablish a right relationship between the refugee and society, drawing back the refugee from bare life and moving forward the community *polis* into communion with the undocumented refugee and with God. Rather than stepping outside the community to live incarnationally, or even in solidarity, with the refugee, as Catholic Social Teaching would describe it,[8] Reformed churches have traditionally sought ways to bring the refugee in from the cold, and back into the common life of society as one who is fully human and loved by God.

Finding a middle ground where God's incarnation and refugee inclusion meet, Christine Pohl interprets radical hospitality as offering the stranger "creature care." She sees Jesus's teaching in Matthew 25:31–46 as a key text for hospitality where Jesus offers the kingdom to those who gave merciful care. Matthew 25, in its broader scriptural context, suggests that Christ comes to us in the

---

8. Hinze, "Straining Towards Solidarity," 168.

A Christian Ethic of Worship, Witness, and Welcome

form of the stranger—and we may not recognize him. Pohl argues convincingly that the possibility of receiving Jesus unawares has intensified and influenced the practice of Christian hospitality in showing charity to the stranger.

As an illustration, Pohl points us to Christmas. In Hispanic communities, Christian congregations reenact the searching by Joseph and Mary to find lodging in Bethlehem in a liturgical tradition called *Las Posadas*. Congregants act out the event by going from house to house in the neighborhood, or from pew to pew in the church. They are categorically denied entrance until the merciful innkeeper is found who allows them a place in the stable yard. The tradition of *Las Posadas*, renewed with each retelling of the Christmas story, and the scriptural reminder of Christ's words "I was a stranger and you invited me in," are vivid biblical affirmations that Christians are called to welcome every stranger, even the undocumented one, as a potential encounter with Christ.[9]

In some ways the Holy Family's searching for shelter in the middle of the night, and the *Posadas* tale of rejection and finally finding sanctuary, prepares the ground for churches' historical tendency to offer sanctuary for people on the run. Church sanctuary is hospitality and political action combined. It is Christian witness to the ethical conviction that the just nation-state should offer protection to the refugee. Churches can move further in welcoming the refugee by advancing from worship and fellowship time to engaging in witness and mission. Witness and mission are ways for congregations to interact with the government of the nation-state in the name of Christ.

CHRISTIAN WITNESSING: ACTS OF ADVOCACY AND SANCTUARY AS PROPHETIC ACTION

Reformed theologian Karl Barth argued that churches have the role of witnessing to God's purposes and against the injustices of civil society—in fact, churches are to be "the model and

---

9. Pohl, *Making Room*, 68.

Part 3: Abiding with the Undocumented Refugee

prototype of the real State."[10] Thus, for the Christian in the Reformed tradition, the church has both a prophetic and a political role: to witness to, advocate for, and model the relationship that the nation-state itself should be providing to the long-term resident undocumented refugee.

Advocacy

Congregants model their faith and provide Christian witness when they visit refugees held in detention, advocate for the constitutional rights of all aliens, including undocumented refugees, and propose changes to immigration laws that provide a path to citizenship for them. Churches and congregations can do this by writing to their representatives in Congress, supporting civil liberties proponents, like the American Civil Liberties Union, that bring lawsuits against perceived unjust actions of government agencies, or joining in rallies and prayer vigils to publicize the threat of bare life existence that beleaguers the neighbor undocumented refugee.

Churches can offer connection and witness by providing or pointing to community resources for jobs, language training, cultural activities, and skills training. Individual congregants can offer assistance with creature care by offering housing, furnishings, food, medical support, clothing, or by providing resources for pursuing legal immigration status, accompaniment to court hearings, and assistance with asylum applications. By engaging with the local *polis* where they reside and partnering with immigrant-led support groups for new immigrants, congregants can make a lasting difference and instigate positive change by grassroots activism on behalf of their undocumented neighbor refugees.

Similarly, church denominational leadership, and interdenominational grassroots groups can, and do, speak out for change through policy statements of their own, Scripture-based letters advocating for greater justice, and support of mission outreach to the refugee left outside the social safety net of our welfare system.

10. Barth, *Community*, 186.

Some denominations, including the Reformed and Lutheran faith traditions, also encourage their member churches to offer sanctuary in their buildings to undocumented refugees fleeing from ICE arrest. Becoming a "sanctuary church" is a radical act of support and welcome. Although harboring undocumented refugees violates immigration laws, it may be possible to provide sanctuary without illegal harboring. Some sanctuary churches proclaim the presence of the undocumented refugee in their halls by public declaration so as not to be accused of hiding them. But the tactic has not been successful when tested in court, and ICE immigration officials retain the power to enter the church premises with a judicial warrant to make arrests at any time.

Sanctuary is far from a perfect means of refugee welcome. Despite denominational leadership in the US expressing support for congregations offering their church spaces as a "sanctuary" for undocumented aliens, living in church sanctuary does not provide a pathway to permanent and legal residency in the US for the long-term resident undocumented refugee. Church sanctuary does not provide the outcome refugees to the US are looking for: a legal and permanent place in the *polis* where they can find protection and peace. And sanctuary violates immigration laws against aiding and abetting aliens who are present in the US without authorization.

As a result of these limitations, congregants and churches should reflect prayerfully on whether sanctuary provides effective assistance to the long-term resident undocumented refugee in their community context. Aliens in the US without documentation need help politically to gain authorized residency status. Each congregation must discern what type of Christian witness will be most effective in achieving the political and theological goal of refugee welcome.

In contemplating God's sovereign laws of peace and justice, congregants may decide that the immigration laws discriminating against long-term resident refugees are so unjust as to merit their civil disobedience of them. If they do, and decide as a church to offer sanctuary, then they will be justified under God's laws, but will have no defense under civil laws. Nevertheless, many church

Part 3: Abiding with the Undocumented Refugee

congregants do decide to violate immigration laws in order to model a more just treatment of the undocumented refugee as a matter of Christian ethics. There are lessons to be learned from the US church sanctuary movement, but also risks involved. Congregants will be helped in their discernment of whether to offer sanctuary by understanding the full picture of the history of church sanctuary in the US and what it means today.

Chapter 6

Sanctuary Church, Civil Disobedience, or Lawful Advocacy?

> "Then the king will say to those at his right hand, 'Come, you that are blessed by my Father, inherit the kingdom prepared for you from the foundation of the world; for I was hungry and you gave me food, I was thirsty and you gave me something to drink, I was a stranger and you welcomed me.'"
>
> —MATT 25:34–35 (NRSV)

SANCTUARY AS CHRISTIAN WITNESS

THE US SANCTUARY MOVEMENT grew out of a long tradition of church sanctuary offered as refuge for wrongdoers fleeing punishment. The church building as a sacred safe space has been

Part 3: Abiding with the Undocumented Refugee

acknowledged since the earliest days of the church. It evolved from even older provisions in Hebrew Scripture that designated sanctuary cities to which aliens could flee in escaping retribution for murder before a trial could be held.[1] The concept of sanctuary churches rose up afresh in the US in the 1980s in order to address the persecution of a particular group fleeing across international borders for safety: the Central American refugee.

In Tucson, Arizona, in the early 1980s, local residents began finding Central American refugees dead and dying in the border desert that stretches from Mexico northward into the US. These were refugees who had escaped on foot the violence of US-backed regimes in their home countries. Indirect US involvement in their persecution fueled the sense of moral outrage felt by the church groups who first came to the aid of these Central American refugees entering the US barely alive. US missionaries returning home from Guatemala and El Salvador confirmed stories of refugees being tortured and murdered by death squads.[2] Quaker Jim Corbett, one of the US sanctuary movement leaders, described the violence in Central America precipitating the refugee crisis as a "full-scale holocaust."[3] In response, he and other church leaders, including Presbyterian pastor Jim Fife, formed the Tucson Ecumenical Council (TEC) to assist the refugees.

They began by working within the bounds of the law, paying bail for arrested refugees and providing them housing on release. Yet the refugees they bailed out were never granted asylum and instead were later rounded up again and deported, discouraging the efforts of their rescuers—and thwarting the hopes of the refugees. Their frustration with the outcome of their legal efforts to assist asylum-seekers led Corbett and Fife, and the other TEC volunteers, to begin implementing alternative means of aiding the refugees. They began "evasion services" of picking up refugees from the desert and driving them around checkpoints by backroads to

---

1. E.g., Num 35:9–12.
2. Cunningham, *God and Caesar*, 23.
3. Golden and McConnell, *Sanctuary*, 47.

safe homes, then housing them in Fife's church sanctuary.[4] Eventually the number of immigrants crossing the desert into Tucson led the TEC and others to develop an underground railroad along a vast church network that spread across the nation, moving refugees from south to north.

In these early days, the church members and others who helped establish a place of "sanctuary" in Fife's church in Tucson, and in private homes, convinced themselves that their actions were legal. They did so by redefining for themselves the terminology used in the US immigration law discourse. For example, they recast the anti-migrant label of "illegal aliens" often applied to immigrants from Central America by renaming them "legal refugees."[5] Never mind that these refugees did not pass US border control to establish for themselves a claim for asylum. The TEC saw the requirement of requesting legal asylum of a border agent as pointless because, they argued, the border agents unfairly rejected the claims the refugees were making during their "credible fear" interviews for asylum.[6] Although they had no legal standing to do so, the TEC's recasting the status of the refugees in terms more congruent with the law helped the TEC members grow their movement.

Civil Initiative as Prophetic Action

Part of TEC's recasting terminology concerning the refugee also included a new way of describing their own work as refugee aid workers. Church workers did not want to commit acts of civil disobedience and the TEC leaders did not want to describe their activities as such. Instead they recast their ministry as a "civil initiative" that the faithful willingly joined in order to be of service to their new immigrant neighbors. Described in this light, congregants saw themselves engaging in the prophetic modelling of a "just state," as Barth encouraged after witnessing the derailment

---

4. Golden and McConnell, *Sanctuary*, 46.
5. Coutin, *The Culture of Protest*, 107.
6. Davis, "A Critical Assessment," 15.

89

Part 3: Abiding with the Undocumented Refugee

of justice under the Nazi regime and the church's failure to act.[7] For the aid workers, joining a "civil initiative" seemed safe, law-abiding, and even patriotic.

Ethnographer Susan Coutin studied the activities of the refugee aid workers in Tucson a decade after it had evolved into a nation-wide sanctuary movement. She interviewed the church workers who pursued this "civil initiative" to bring refugees into the US, shelter them, and publicize their stories in order to protest the US government's immigration policies towards refugees. Based on the workers' interactions with immigration officials, Coutin noticed that sanctuary workers developed a "legal consciousness" by which they made and pursued their own interpretations of law. They used the term "civil initiative" rather than "civil disobedience" in order to perpetuate a sense of compliance, or at least willingness to remain within the bounds of the law, and to extend it where they saw its inadequacies. They argued that if migrants merited asylum, they were "refugees" regardless of whether a US immigration official had declared them as such. They saw it as a citizen's duty to enforce the laws (of providing asylum) if the government fails to do so.[8]

These efforts of creating a civil initiative to protect the Central American refugee are impressive in that the sanctuary workers in Tucson, and later in the East Bay of San Francisco and Chicago, went to great lengths to promote their actions as being legal. Once they established for themselves that the Central Americans were refugees, the sanctuary workers took the next step of arguing that sheltering, assisting, and transporting the refugees, "even in face of government opposition, *obeyed*, rather than violated, the law."[9] Although these arguments were a comfort to the sanctuary workers, they did not stand up well in a court of law.

In January 1985 sixteen members of the Tucson sanctuary workers group, including founders of the TEC, Corbett and Fife, were indicted for crimes of conspiracy, bringing aliens illegally into

7. Barth, *Community*, 186–87.
8. Coutin, *The Culture of Protest*, 108–9.
9. Coutin, *The Culture of Protest*, 109, emphasis in the original.

Sanctuary Church, Civil Disobedience, or Lawful Advocacy?

the US, aiding and harboring undocumented aliens, and other violations of US immigration laws. A jury found guilty all but three of the sanctuary worker defendants. The convicted church workers were given suspended sentences with three to five years' probation.[10] The trial attracted national attention as a clash of religion against the nation-state where the raw tension between church and state was awkwardly held at bay in a tightly managed courtroom. The defendant church workers' "civil initiative" way of thinking, permitting an inductive measure of what the law should be, one that coincided with their religious and humanitarian views, created an uneasy tension and an untenable legal argument. To the trial judge in Tucson, sanctuary was a blatant violation of the law and an effort by individual church leaders to define the law for themselves.[11]

Significantly, Rev. Fife's own reflections on his "civil initiative" to aid the undocumented refugee do not suggest a man who arrogantly snubbed the law or saw himself as above the law. Rather, he was willing to claim God's sovereignty as overarching and the claims of Christ as taking precedence over all else. In a lecture Fife gave after the trial in 1988 at Princeton Theological Seminary, he commented that his civil initiative of sanctuary in Tucson was very much a Christian ethical act, applying the law of welcome for refugees fleeing persecution. He saw it as a moral imperative to help refugees evade the alleged illegal efforts of the US government to return refugees to the dangers of their home countries.

Fife argued passionately that "the faith communities must act to protect the refugee when the State does not" because God calls us to serve a greater good, to lift up the neighbor refugee, and show mercy. If the nation-state refuses to do so, the church must. "In all the world," Fife declared, "there is no other institution for defending human rights in refugees' lives, other than communities of faith . . . The church must embody a commitment to transcend national duties to civil obedience."[12] For Fife, who was actively rescuing refugees from the death squads rampant in

---

10. Cunningham, *God and Caesar*, 59.
11. Cunningham, *God and Caesar*, 59.
12. Fife, "Prophetic Community," audio, 54:30.

Part 3: Abiding with the Undocumented Refugee

Central America in the 1980s, civil "initiative" was both, in his view, a faith requirement and a legal obligation. He argued that the US Declaration of Independence identified certain inalienable rights, such as the preservation of life, that no government can rescind, and if it does, its efforts are illegitimate, and the government cannot force its citizens to submit to them. He looked to the rulings of the Courts of Nuremberg that established the notion that every individual is responsible to defend human rights, even when a nation-state's "orders or obligations compel their violation."[13]

Rev. John Fife and the members of the interfaith TEC lived in a community next to the border walls of the nation-state where the welcome of refugees was an immediate matter of life or death. Decades later, how do we approach the sons and daughters of these refugees, the ones who made it inside our bordered territory, but still live outside our civil laws? Is prolonged church sanctuary the answer, or is there something else for churches and congregants to do to help the long-term resident, undocumented refugee become a full member of society?

Civil Disobedience in the Reformed Tradition

Arguably, civil disobedience, such as the TEC's civil initiatives and "sanctuary church," should be an action of last resort in the Reformed faith tradition. For the refugee aid workers in Tucson in the early 1980s, it *was* the last resort—and very much a higher calling. Today's churches considering sanctuary as a way of welcoming their long-term, undocumented resident refugee neighbors face a different context. The long-term undocumented refugees are settled. They have shelter and jobs. The task for congregants and churches today is to understand the needs of their neighbor undocumented refugees as being political, not humanitarian, and discern how they might help them meet their political needs through Christ-inspired action. To welcome undocumented

---

13. Fife, "Prophetic Community."

Sanctuary Church, Civil Disobedience, or Lawful Advocacy?

refugees into the *polis*, citizens must help them become legal members of it. Doing so legally may be the most effective means to help.

Churches in the Presbyterian-Reformed tradition should consider whether civil disobedience is ever an ethical response to laws that disfavor the long-term resident undocumented refugee. The Reformed faith encourages a certain level of partnership with civil authority, respect and deference for magistrates (even despotic ones),[14] and recognition of the *polis* as part of God's overall provision for our peaceful earthly existence. Calvin cautioned against private individuals violating the authority of magistrates, elected, or selected officials. He described them as being "full of venerable majesty, which God has established by the weightiest decrees, even though it may reside with the most unworthy men."[15]

Yet Calvin also affirms that we ultimately must follow our Christian conscience when faced by unjust civil strictures. He concludes that:

> Obedience due [to the authority of rulers] . . . is never to lead us away from obedience to [God] to whose decrees all their commands ought to yield, to whose majesty their scepters ought to be submitted . . . The Lord therefore is the King of Kings.[16]

In brief, obedience to God comes first, but tolerance of the unjust ruler, and patience in persevering, is also a prerequisite part of the Reformed Christian life.

The questions for congregants to examine in discerning the best approach for church advocacy should be specific to each local congregation. Congregants should be asking themselves and discussing together where they stand on questions such as these: "What means of advocacy for my neighbor, undocumented resident refugees, are most effective and meaningful for restoring them to full humanity as a member of my local community at the present time? How can I make a difference that helps improve

---

14. Calvin, *Institutes* IV.xx.24–26:1511–14.
15. Calvin, *Institutes* IV.xx.31:1518.
16. Calvin, *Institutes* IV.xx.32:1520.

Part 3: Abiding with the Undocumented Refugee

their chances to reside legally here? How can I help them in their everyday lives—to be more included in the church community, and the broader local *polis*, and to enjoy a full and dignified human existence as my neighbor?" Outlined below are two directions that congregants and churches might choose to follow depending on their context, and the needs of their neighbor refugees.

CHOICES FOR CHURCHES IN WELCOMING THE RESIDENT UNDOCUMENTED REFUGEE

Having established ways to welcome the long-term resident undocumented refugee through worship and witness, I present solutions that churches and congregants can implement as they determine the kind of welcome of the undocumented refugee that is most appropriate for their sense of Christian calling in their community context. Given our learning about the spectrum of ethical Christian viewpoints on the morality of border walls, and the tension in our immigration law and alienage law framework that leaves many refugees bereft of a path to legal residency, even if they entered the country legally when first seeking asylum, we know that there is more than one ethically just result for the ways churches and congregants can offer welcome.

To aid further in that discernment, I offer examples of two potential outcomes based on a church's assessment of its call to welcome the long-term resident refugee. These practical action plans each embody a Christian ethic of loving one's neighbor in need, based on a church's self-understanding of its role in supporting a just immigration ethic for undocumented refugees. These approaches are (i) civil disobedience through a "new" sanctuary movement and (ii) political advocacy within the law.

Different congregations will land on different places along the spectrum of ways to welcome the neighbor. But just as we saw in discerning a political theology of cosmopolitanism or communitarianism within an understanding of a just Christian immigration ethic for border walls, there is a palette of practical choices for churches and congregants to make in discerning what an ethic of

Sanctuary Church, Civil Disobedience, or Lawful Advocacy?

Christian hospitality might look like in their own neighborhoods. Among "Reformed churches always reforming," one size does not fit all, nor is one solution always and forever the most apt.

Civil Disobedience and the New Sanctuary Movement

As a threshold matter, congregants contemplating acts of civil disobedience must ask themselves: "At what point do we break the law in order to change the law?" This discernment process is a necessary first step for every congregation. Even the most law-abiding and risk-averse congregations can sometimes surprise themselves when prayerfully reflecting on the question that can save the life of the refugee.[17] Sanctuary protects the undocumented alien, temporarily, and can raise consciousness about the legal injustice they face. But church sanctuary, outside of life-or-death situations, like survival in the Arizona desert,[18] may not be the most effective form of assistance to the refugee in areas with more moderate climates and alternative resources. In forming a Christian ethic of hospitality to welcome the undocumented refugee, every church must decide for itself whether civil disobedience is necessary to bear witness to God's sovereign will and gospel promise.

When we meet our undocumented refugee neighbors who have long since settled into the community, no longer facing a day-to-day life-or-death survival situation, radical acts of civil disobedience, even if called civil initiatives, are arguably less needful. Sanctuary, when offered as no more than harboring refugees, is less helpful to them. The social limitations of living confined in a church building can be injurious emotionally to the refugee over several weeks or months there. Although sanctuary may have some brief utility in thwarting instances of hot pursuit by ICE agents, it is not a permanent method for fostering a flourishing life. There

---

17. For testimonial examples of this transformative change in congregations, see Golden and McConnell, *Sanctuary*, 132–33. Also see, Coutin, *The Culture of Protest*, 66. And see Hallie, *Lest Innocent Blood Be Shed.*

18. Cunningham, *God and Caesar*, xiii. Also see, Golden and McConnell, *Sanctuary*, 14–15.

Part 3: Abiding with the Undocumented Refugee

needs to be a next step—a political step—that restores the refugee to full membership in the community with a legal status consistent with long-term, peaceful residency.

Some of the key issues for congregants to weigh in their discernment of whether to offer sanctuary are the survival risks to the refugee if deported, the rupture to family in the US whether living in the church or removed from the country, and the means of finding alternative living arrangements for the refugee, even transferring the refugee to a new jurisdiction. The need of the undocumented refugee is not housing. It's political. The refugee is seeking a legal place in the *polis*. For many refugees, taking sanctuary in a church may prove to be a counterproductive measure in meeting that goal.

Forty years after the US sanctuary movement first began in the Arizona desert, a "new sanctuary movement" focuses more on immigrant-led initiatives, interfaith partnerships, and justice-seeking with long-term goals of freedom and human dignity for all refugees, regardless of their status. One example can be found in the New Sanctuary Movement in Philadelphia and other coalition partners throughout the northeast. Organized by first generation immigrants working on behalf of new immigrants, inviting communities of faith to partner with them, the New Sanctuary Movement of Philadelphia has gained traction as a grassroots, politically focused group seeking changes to unjust immigration laws and their implementation. They seek political permanency in the US for all undocumented immigrants.

The organizers see their efforts theologically and practically. The New Sanctuary Movement of Philadelphia describes sanctuary in broader terms than offering protective housing in a church, although they include that too, when necessary. As a local activism effort, they successfully encouraged the Philadelphia Police Department to refuse enforcement assistance to federal ICE agents, resulting in Philadelphia becoming a "sanctuary city" in 2014. The group's statement on sanctuary describes a vision of building a sanctuary world.[19]

19. For more information about the New Sanctuary Movement in

Sanctuary Church, Civil Disobedience, or Lawful Advocacy?

Their cosmopolitan dream includes all people and is legitimized by elements of faith-based partnering and immigrant inclusion in the leadership of the organization itself. It successfully resolves the issues of white paternalism and male-dominated leadership that beleaguered the Tucson/East Bay/Chicago sanctuary movements of the 1980s.[20] Acknowledging the need for collaboration, the New Sanctuary Movement of Philadelphia has been co-directed by a man and a woman, since its founding over a decade ago. Co-director Blanca Pacheco is an immigrant herself.

There are many ways to witness to Christ's mercy for the stranger. Sanctuary protection in a church may not be the answer if it merely isolates the undocumented refugee and does nothing to improve legal status or secure belonging in the community. If the threat of deportation is at stake, legal representation, public advocacy, group accompaniment to meetings with ICE, all have greater appeal. Learning from the sanctuary challenges of the past, The New Sanctuary Movement of Philadelphia has embraced this advocacy role, identifying itself as "an interfaith, multicultural immigrant justice movement organizing communities to end injustices against immigrants, regardless of status."[21] And while the New Sanctuary Movement in Philadelphia does support traditional sanctuary in churches for immigrants seeking refuge, its focus is more on systemic change, revision of federal immigration laws, and creating a world of safety for all.

The sanctuary movement has never been without conflict. For some churches, providing sanctuary may be a step too far; for others it will feel like a necessary next step. The decisive factor will be the work of the Spirit in the hearts and minds of the congregation. But for those churches who join the sanctuary movement and have achieved a sense of solidarity with the refugee, these challenges are mere inconveniences to be addressed. For them, offering church sanctuary to their neighbor, undocumented refugee may be the capstone of their discipleship and their most courageous and

---

Philadelphia, see its website at www.sanctuaryphiladelphia.org.

20. Golden and McConnell, *Sanctuary*, 54–55, 59–62.
21. New Sanctuary Movement of Philadelphia, "Who We Are."

Part 3: Abiding with the Undocumented Refugee

authentic expression of a Christian ethic of hospitality towards the undocumented refugee.

Political Activism within the Legal Bounds of the Nation-State

Many congregants and churches conclude that they can make a bigger impact on rectifying injustices facing refugees by working within the bounds of the civil justice system and legislative procedure. Churches that choose legal advocacy can pursue traditional lobbying efforts of letter-writing, phone calls, and visits to federal congressional representatives to advocate for an amnesty program for the long-term refugee, or changes in the immigration laws that provide a path to citizenship for undocumented refugees after living for a certain period of time in the US.

In order to meet the refugee neighbor in need and offer hospitality through worship and welcome, churches can partner with local organizations like the immigrant-led Community Resource Center (CRC) in New York's Westchester County that works to assist new immigrants, regardless of legal status, with support and information.[22] CRC is led by its executive director, Jirandy Martinez, the daughter of an immigrant herself, and an effective partner with local churches in the area that provide volunteer support and charitable giving. One area of compassionate volunteerism that the CRC organizes is an accompaniment program for undocumented immigrants called to report to ICE hearings or registration check-ins. Being present with the neighbor refugee in confronting the US legal system provides solidarity and raises the refugee's spirits. Political advocacy, one on one, can look like compassionate, pastoral care.

The strength of political advocacy comes in multiplying grassroots efforts through numbers of participants. When churches organize congregation-wide letter writing campaigns, politicians receive higher volumes of demands from the constituents they represent—and whose votes they want to retain. Churches who

---

22. To read more about the Community Resource Center, visit their website at https://www.crcny.org/.

Sanctuary Church, Civil Disobedience, or Lawful Advocacy?

partner with community organizations learn what is most helpful and relevant to their neighborhood refugee. Sometimes the simple act of regular financial support of local immigrant organizations can have the biggest impact on successful integration of undocumented refugees into community life. Collaborating on social media publicity campaigns that lobby for law changes or legal defense funding can quickly build a significant coalition to pressure legislators, seek release of detained long-term resident refugees, and raise the consciousness of others in the *polis* who might not be church members but who take an interest in the justice issues at stake.

For churches that wish to remain within the scope of civil law but also see the long-term resident undocumented refugee as a neighbor in need, they can start with welcome, worship, and witness. While lobbying for long-term legislative change, congregants can also provide creature care in the short term. They can provide material goods needed by indigent refugees who have fallen outside of the social welfare nets of society. Offering access to food pantries, rides to medical appointments, clothing distribution, school backpacks and supplies, and assistance with job applications and obtaining driver's licenses, churches and congregants can make a difference in the lives of their neighbors here and now. Grassroots refugee-aid organizations around the country offer volunteer opportunities and training that also includes legal assistance with asylum applications and courtroom accompaniment. Church leaders can be researching what advocacy groups are already present in their midst.

In making connections with the neighbor refugee, churches and congregants can discover the blessing of receiving the stranger through the gifts of their different culture, language, and way of being. Many congregants find that they receive more back than they give out in welcoming their neighbors in need. For many churches, welcoming the undocumented refugee as a neighbor is a means of expanding the community, and normalizing the existence of those whom the law does not recognize, but whom Christ does. Working within the laws and norms of civil society requires ongoing advocacy over long periods of time. It may take years to

Part 3: Abiding with the Undocumented Refugee

change US law or immigration policy, but it only takes a matter of a fellowship meal, a shared communion, and a conversation with the neighbor refugee to make an immediate difference in our common life together.

SUMMARY OF PART 3

Part 3 of this book outlined a practical theology of refugee neighbor welcome for churches and congregants to consider implementing in full or in part. It provided practical approaches to helping the undocumented refugee feel included in the community beginning with the worship of God and extending out to the love of neighbor through political advocacy and witness. Having equipped churches and congregants to see their undocumented refugee neighbors as a vulnerable group, one that even US alienage law recognizes as having certain rights, a group in need of a peaceful polity, these chapters offered concrete ways for congregants to embody refugee welcome through worship and witness.

For some churches, worship leads to fellowship and connection, fertile ground for neighborly assistance and a starting place for enlarging the community to include the refugee. Other congregations will be inspired to embrace modes of political advocacy, working to change the laws that prevent resident undocumented refugees from becoming citizens or legal resident aliens. In instances when the neighbor refugee is under threat of arrest and *refoulement*, where the legal environment has disintegrated to the point of reducing the resident refugee to a bare life existence, churches may feel called to offer "sanctuary," or engage in other acts of civil disobedience in order to preserve the life of the undocumented refugee. These are decisions to be made individually and prayerfully, informed by the context in which congregants and their refugee neighbors live.

The witness of the church is always to uphold and enlarge the laws of a peaceful society. Life in a peaceful *polis* is the greatest need of the refugee. The Reformed tradition supports civil laws and revisions to them, having always seen itself as the church

Sanctuary Church, Civil Disobedience, or Lawful Advocacy?

"reformed and ever reforming," making space for evolving practices in response to God's evolving world. There is no one right answer to neighbor welcome, but there are methods of analysis, consistency of purpose, and an ever-present reminder for churches and congregants to operate with their eyes on Christ. This Christ-centered *telos* commits us to pursue one goal: the communion of all humanity, in all its diversity, with God. We can begin to realize this sacred goal in our everyday lives, in partnership with the *polis*, by promoting the human flourishing of all people for the common good. Welcoming the undocumented resident refugee as neighbor in Christ is one step forward along this path.

Conclusion

THIS BOOK INTRODUCED A discernment process based in political theology and Christian ethics for congregants and churches to apply in addressing the question of neighbor love for the long-term US resident undocumented refugee living in their communities. Using the Reformed faith tradition as our methodology, we began by addressing the question of the morality of bordered walls, and then undertook a comparative study of the laws of the nation-state and the sovereignty of God and their impact on the refugee. We grew to understand the undocumented refugee as God's beloved creation, as an unauthorized resident alien, and as a protected person living near, to whom we owe a duty of neighbor love.

Analyzing the question of migration control at the borders of the nation-state as it affects refugees informs congregants about the special duty of care towards refugees and the bare life existence they face. Beyond humanitarian concerns, Christian ethics teaches us that the needs of the refugee are political, first and foremost. The refugee and the citizen also share the same political goal of living in a peaceful community with protection and stability provided by the nation-state, where they can flourish in a common life together, achieving God's greater purposes as well.

Our inquiry has revealed that there are some protections for the resident refugee in the United States by virtue of provisions of the US Constitution that apply to all persons, aliens, in particular, who are US residents but not US citizens. These special protections,

Conclusion

promising the alien due process at law, bail hearings, and nondiscrimination, elevate the refugee from bare life to something more: political personhood. While personhood does not achieve the benefits of citizenship, it does offer the undocumented refugee dignity as well as certain legal protections due all people as a human right and a minimal level of community acknowledgment.

Churches and congregations can help undocumented resident refugees to become legal members of the community by serving as their advocates and being their voices in the communities where they have none. Outsiders, like the undocumented refugee, might experience churches as a place to worship and find communion with God, for faith fellowship, and human connection. Church communities can provide this place of belonging for the undocumented refugee even while the *polis* tells them they do not belong at all.

There is no one right pathway to welcoming in our near neighbors. Every church and congregant must discern the welcome that best suits their own community context. Some may offer welcome within the limits of the law, through lobbying politicians for changes to the laws on immigration, assisting with legal filings for asylum and court hearings, offering hospitality through creature care and kindness, or fellowship and worship welcome. Others may determine that the injustices to the undocumented refugee have become too great, their due process rights have been denied, and the risk of their being returned to their home countries where their lives are in danger is a constant threat. For these congregants and churches, they may choose civil disobedience as their way of assisting the undocumented refugee.

But so long as injustices can be rectified by legal means, and the US remains a democratic republic governed by the rule of law, advocating for changes in immigration law and policy is the most effective political action to assist the undocumented alien. The Reformed tradition would recommend working to change the system from within to make lasting changes that would open paths to citizenship for the long-term resident, undocumented refugee. I support this studied approach to legislative change as well.

Conclusion

I conclude with a call to action: for congregations to reach out to meet their neighbors, the undocumented, often invisible, resident alien refugees living among them. Welcome them to church, offer them connection, show hospitality, and hear their stories. Working together, churches and refugees can restore justice, find forgiveness, and advocate for legislation that provides a path towards legalized status for the undocumented refugee. As Christians, we are called to welcome the stranger with loving kindness and show mercy to our neighbors in need. To do so, we must keep Christ at our center, the one who welcomes everyone to the table, including the undocumented refugee, hungry to belong.

Epilogue

THE DAY BEFORE THANKSGIVING, November 25, 2018, Roby was allowed a bail hearing by a federal court judge for the first time. He had been held in an ICE detention facility for ten months. The judge released him on $1,000 bail which was paid by a legal defense fund set up by members of his congregation. He had to wear an ankle monitor to track his whereabouts at all times. But he was home for Thanksgiving. Rejoined with his wife and two daughters at long last in their modest New Jersey apartment, Roby gave thanks to God, and to all the people in his church community who helped him and his family throughout his detention. "Thanks be to God," Roby told me when we spoke by phone once he was back on the "outside"—he was choking back tears.

Roby still awaits the outcome of his asylum case. With the help of the ACLU and the *pro bono* services of a major New York law firm, in May 2019 a federal court granted a humanitarian petition made on his behalf to remove his ankle monitor permanently. The federal government also renewed his work permit and returned to him his driver's license, although he is still required to report to ICE every six months.

In June 2021, advocates for undocumented refugees were successful in persuading the State of New Jersey to prohibit federal homeland security's ICE agents from using the Essex County detention center, where Roby had been held, to detain undocumented aliens in the future. The multistory penitentiary will no

Epilogue

longer house undocumented refugees and others present in the US without authorization. But, unfortunately, ICE detainees arrested in New Jersey will be sent to other states for detention, far from their families and attorney representation.

Advocates for detainees had hoped the detentions of undocumented people would stop altogether. They argued that living in the US without authorization is a civil wrong not a criminal matter. When the Biden administration took office in January 2021, the acting secretary of the Department of Homeland Security issued a memo on new immigration enforcement priorities that directed ICE to limit arrests and detainment to only those individuals who pose a threat to national security, border security, and public safety. Since then, advocates for undocumented refugees across the country have argued that ICE is not implementing those guidelines.

But Roby made it out in time. He went back to work and safely settled in with his family at home. He is still under surveillance. He cannot travel by plane and has no passport. He is stateless; but in the US, he has personhood. He is more than bare life. He is loved by his community and his congregation. And he never lost his faith in God.

Bibliography

Agamben, Giorgio. *Homo Sacer: Sovereign Power and Bare Life*. Translated by Daniel Heller-Roazen. Stanford, CA: Stanford University Press, 1998.
Ahn, Ilsup. *Religious Ethics and Migration: Doing Justice to Undocumented Workers*. New York: Routledge, 2014.
Amstutz, Mark R. *Just Immigration: American Policy in Christian Perspective*. Grand Rapids: Eerdmans, 2017.
Arendt, Hannah. *The Origins of Totalitarianism*. New York: Harvest/Houghton Mifflin Harcourt, 1976 (1951).
Ashworth, Justin P. "Who Are Our People? Toward a Christian Witness against Borders." *Modern Theology* 34, no. 4 (2018) 495–518.
Augustine. *Concerning the City of God against the Pagans*. Translated by Henry Bettenson. London: Penguin, 2003.
———. *De Doctrina Christiana*. Translated by R. P. H. Green. Oxford: Oxford University Press, 1995.
Barth, Karl. *Church Dogmatics*. Translated by G. T. Thomson et al. Edinburgh: T. & T. Clark, 1936–77.
———. *Community, State, and Church*. Introduction by David Haddorff. Eugene, OR: Wipf & Stock, 2004 (1960).
Barth, Karl, et al. "The Theological Declaration of Barmen 1934." Reprinted in *The Book of Confessions, The Constitution of the Presbyterian Church (USA), Part 1*, 280–84. Louisville: The Office of the General Assembly, 2016.
Benedict, Philip. "Calvin and the Transformation of Geneva." In *John Calvin's Impact on Church and Society 1509–2009*, edited by Martin Ernst Hirzel and Martin Sallman, 1–13. Grand Rapids: Eerdmans, 2009.
Bosniak, Linda. *The Citizen and the Alien: Dilemmas of Contemporary Membership*. Princeton, NJ: Princeton University Press, 2006.
Bretherton, Luke. *Christ and the Common Life: Political Theology and the Case for Democracy*. Grand Rapids: Eerdmans, 2019.
———. *Christianity and Contemporary Politics: The Conditions and Possibilities of Faithful Witness*. Malden, MA: Wiley-Blackwell, 2010.

Bibliography

———. "The Duty of Care to Refugees, Christian Cosmopolitanism, and the Hallowing of Bare Life." *Studies in Christian Ethics* 19, no. 1 (April 2006) 39–61.

———. "The End of National Borders: Thinking Ethically in the Face of Mass Migration." *ABC Religion and Ethics* (May 20, 2015). http://www.abc.net.au/religion/articles/2015/05/20/4239083.htm.

———. *Hospitality as Holiness: Christian Witness amid Moral Diversity*. Surrey: Ashgate, 2006.

Bullinger, Heinrich. "Second Helvetic Confession." Reprinted in *Book of Confessions Constitution of the Presbyterian Church (USA), Part I*, 75–143. Louisville: Office of the General Assembly, Presbyterian Church (USA), 2016.

Calvin, John. *Institutes of the Christian Religion*, Vols. I & II. Edited by John T. McNeill. Translated by Ford Lewis Battles. Louisville: Westminster John Knox, 1960.

Carens, Joseph H. "Aliens and Citizens: The Case for Open Borders." *The Review of Politics* 49, no. 2 (Spring 1987) 251–73.

———. *The Ethics of Immigration*. Oxford: Oxford University Press, 2013.

———. *Immigrants and the Right to Stay*. Cambridge, MA: MIT Press, 2010.

Catholic Church and Conferencia del Episcopado Mexicano, eds. *Strangers No Longer: Together on the Journey of Hope: A Pastoral Letter Concerning Migration*. Washington, DC: United States Conference of Catholic Bishops, 2003.

Collier, Elizabeth W., and Charles R. Strain, with Catholic Relief Services. *Global Migration: What's Happening, Why, and a Just Response*. Winona, MN: Anselm Academic, 2017.

Coutin, Susan Bibler. *The Culture of Protest: Religious Activism and the U.S. Sanctuary Movement*. Boulder, CO: Westview, 1993.

Cunningham, Hilary. *God and Caesar at the Rio Grande: Sanctuary and the Politics of Religion*. Minneapolis: University of Minnesota Press, 1995.

Daniels, Roger. *Guarding the Golden Door: American Immigration Policy and Immigrants since 1882*. New York: Hill and Wang, 2005.

Davis, William J.. "A Critical Assessment of the Sanctuary Argument—Remarks by William J. Davis, S.J." In *Sanctuary: Challenge to the Churches*, edited by Maria H. Thomas, 10–17. Washington, DC: The Institute on Religion and Democracy, 1986.

Elshtain, Jean Bethke. *Sovereignty: God, State, and Self*. New York: Basic, 2008.

Engammare, Max. "Une Certaine Idée de la France chez Calvin l'Exilé." *Bulletin de la Société de l'Histoire du Protestantisme Français* 155, no. 19 (2009) 15–27.

Fife, John M., "Prophetic Community and Civil Initiative." Lecture given at Princeton Theological Seminary, March 7, 1988. Recording and transcription available at http://commons.ptsem.edu/id/01974.

Golden, Renny, and Michael McConnell. *Sanctuary: The New Underground Railroad*. Maryknoll, NY: Orbis, 1986.

Guthrie, Shirley C., Jr. *Always Being Reformed: Faith for a Fragmented World*. Louisville: Westminster John Knox, 2008.

Bibliography

Hallie, Philip. *Lest Innocent Blood Be Shed: The Story of the Village of Le Chambon and How Goodness Happened There.* New York: First Harper Perennial Edition, 1994.

Hauerwas, Stanley. *A Community of Character: Toward A Constructive Social Ethic.* Notre Dame: University of Notre Dame Press, 1981.

———. *After Christendom?* Nashville: Abingdon, 1991.

———. *Vision and Virtue.* Notre Dame: University of Notre Dame Press, 1981 (1974).

Hauerwas, Stanley, and William H. Willimon. *Resident Aliens: Life in the Christian Colony.* Expanded 25th Anniversary Edition. Nashville, TN: Abingdon, 2014.

Heimburger, Robert W. *God and the Illegal Alien: United States Immigration Law and a Theology of Politics.* Law and Christianity. Cambridge: Cambridge University Press, 2018.

Hinze, Christine Firer. "Straining Towards Solidarity in a Suffering World." In *Vatican II: Forty Years Later*, edited by William Madges, 165–95. College Theology Society. Vol. 51. Maryknoll, NY: Orbis, 2005.

Kraus, Hans-Joachim. "The Contemporary Relevance of Calvin's Theology." In *Toward the Future of Reformed Theology*, edited by David Willis and Michael Welker, 323–38. Grand Rapids: Eerdmans, 1999.

Link, Christian. "Election and Predestination." In *John Calvin's Impact on Church and Society, 1509–2009*, edited by Martin Ernst Hirzel and Martin Sallmann, 105–21. Grand Rapids: Eerdmans, 2009.

McKim, Donald K. *Introducing the Reformed Faith.* Louisville: Westminster John Knox, 2001.

———. *Presbyterian Faith that Lives Today.* Louisville: Geneva, 2014.

Meilaender, Peter C. *Toward a Theory of Immigration.* New York: Palgrave, 2001.

New Sanctuary Movement of Philadelphia. "Who We Are." https://www.sanctuaryphiladelphia.org/who-we-are-new-sanctuary/.

Ngai, Mae M. *Impossible Subjects: Illegal Aliens and the Making of Modern America, Updated Edition.* Rev. ed. Princeton, NJ: Princeton University Press, 2014.

Oberman, Heiko A. "*Initia Calvini*: The Matrix of Calvin's Reformation." In *Calvinus Sacrae Scripturae Professor*, compiled by Wilhelm H. Neuser from International Congress on Calvin Research, Aug. 20–23, 1990, 113–54. Grand Rapids: Eerdmans, 1990.

O'Neill, William R. "The Place of Displacement: The Ethics of Migration in the United States." In *Living with(out) Borders: Catholic Theological Ethics on the Migration of Peoples*, edited by Agnes M. Brazal and Maria Teresa Davila, 67–77. Catholic Theological Ethics in the World Church, no. 4. Maryknoll, NY: Orbis, 2016.

Pohl, Christine D. *Making Room: Recovering Hospitality as a Christian Tradition.* Grand Rapids: Eerdmans, 1999.

Pope Pius XII. "Exsul Familia Nazarethana." *Acta Apotolicae Sedis*, XLIV, August 1952. https://www.papalencyclicals.net/pius12/p12exsul.htm.

Bibliography

Presbyterian Church (USA). "Directory for Worship." In *Constitution of the Presbyterian Church (USA), Part II, Book of Order*, 73–117. Louisville: Office of the General Assembly, Presbyterian Church (USA), 2016.

Rajendra, Tisha M. *Migrants and Citizens: Justice and Responsibility in the Ethics of Immigration*. Grand Rapids: Eerdmans, 2017.

Reed, Esther D. *Theology for International Law*. London: Bloomsbury T. & T. Clark, 2013.

Reid, W. Stanford. "John Calvin, Lawyer and Legal Reformer." In *Articles on Calvin and Calvinism*, Vol. I: *The Biography of Calvin*, edited by Richard C. Gamble, 57–72. New York: Garland, 1992.

Rosario Rodríguez, Rubén. "Calvin's Legacy of Compassion: A Reformed Theological Perspective on Immigration." In *Immigrant Neighbors among Us: Immigration across Theological Traditions*, edited by M. Daniel Carroll R. and Leopoldo A. Sánchez M., 44–62. Eugene, OR: Pickwick, 2015.

Singer, Peter. *One World: The Ethics of Globalization*. New Haven, CT: Yale University Press, 2002.

Tichenor, Daniel J. *Dividing Lines: The Politics of Immigration Control in America*. Princeton, NJ: Princeton University Press, 2002.

United Nations High Commissioner for Refugees (UNHCR). "Convention and Protocol Relating to the Status of Refugees." Adopted July 28, 1951. https://www.unhcr.org/en-us/3b66c2aa10.

U.S. Congress. 96 Cong. 2nd Session. "Refugee Act of 1980." U.S. Public Law 96–212. March 17, 1980. https://www.govinfo.gov/content/pkg/STATUTE-94/pdf/STATUTE-94-Pg102.pdf.

U.S. House. 104 Cong. 2nd Session. "H.R. 104–828, to accompany H.R. 2202, Illegal Immigration Reform and Immigrant Responsibility Act of 1996." September 24, 1996. https://www.congress.gov/104/crpt/hrpt828/CRPT-104hrpt828.pdf.

———. 82 Cong. 1st Session. "H.R. 2580, Immigration and Nationality Act of 1965." January 15, 1965. https://www.uscis.gov/legal-resources/immigration-and nationality-act.

Walzer, Michael. *Spheres of Justice: A Defense of Pluralism and Equality*. New York: Basic, 1983.

Wells, Samuel. *God's Companions*. Malden, MA: Blackwell, 2016.

Zachman, Randall C. "John Calvin." In *Reformed Theology*, edited by Paul T. Nimmo and David A. S. Fergusson, 132–47. Cambridge: Cambridge University Press, 2016.

www.ingramcontent.com/pod-product-compliance
Lightning Source LLC
Chambersburg PA
CBHW020854160426
43192CB00007B/922